SCIENTIFIC AMERICAN EXPLORES BIG IDEAS

The Future of Space Exploration

Published in 2027 by Scientific American Educational Publishing
in association with **The Rosen Publishing Group**
2544 Clinton Street, Buffalo NY 14224

Contains material from Scientific American®, a division of Springer Nature America, Inc., reprinted by permission, as well as original material from The Rosen Publishing Group®.

First Edition

Scientific American
Lisa Pallatroni: Project Editor

Rosen Publishing
Nicole Horning: Compiling Editor
Michael Moy: Senior Graphic Designer

Cataloging-in-Publication Data
Names: Scientific American, Inc.
Title: The future of space exploration / edited by the Scientific American Editors.
Description: Buffalo, New York : Scientific American Educational Publishing, an imprint of Rosen Publishing, 2027. | Series: Scientific American explores big ideas | Includes glossary and index.
Identifiers: ISBN 9781538314739 (pbk.) | ISBN 9781538314746 (library bound) | ISBN 9781538314753 (ebook)
Subjects: LCSH: Outer space–Exploration–Juvenile literature. | Space probes–Juvenile literature. | Space colonies–Juvenile literature. | Habitable planets–Juvenile literature. | Space flight–Juvenile literature.
Classification: LCC QB500.22 F888 2027 | DDC 629.435–dc23

Manufactured in the United States of America
Websites listed were live at the time of publication.

Cover: Alones/Shutterstock.com

CPSIA Compliance Information: Batch # CS27SA.
For Further Information contact Rosen Publishing at 1-800-237-9932.

CONTENTS

INTRODUCTION

Space is vast, mysterious, and still largely unknown. But how far can we go? What does it take to explore beyond Earth and who decides what comes next? While space may seem limitless, the future of exploring it is determined by limits here on Earth. Budgets, politics, and global priorities all have a hand in deciding which missions move forward.

Every space mission builds on the last. Scientists and engineers study what has worked, what hasn't, and what was discovered, and then use this information to improve future missions. From launching satellites to sending astronauts into space, each step helps us better understand how to explore safely and what comes next. But progress is about more than science. It also depends on funding and political decisions that can change over time.

This book is a collection of articles that explore what lies ahead in space exploration and the challenges that come with it. In Handling Space Debris, you'll learn about the growing problem of objects left behind in space and how they can be dealt with. From there, you'll explore missions that have been taken into space as well as future missions. In Living on Other Planets, you'll learn more about a discussion: Is it possible to live on other planets, and what are the challenges of this? After learning about living in space, you'll discover the possibility of other life in space with Alien Lifeforms. Finally, in The Politics of the Future of Space Exploration, we look at how budgets and recent politics are impacting space missions and research.

What comes next in space exploration depends on more than just curiosity. Advances in science and technology must work with funding, decision-making, politics, and other challenges. Together, these challenges will influence how far, fast, and responsibly people can continue to explore beyond Earth.

Section 1: Handling Space Debris

Plans to Trash the Space Station Preview a Bigger Problem

By Sarah Scoles

If you're hanging out near the Pacific Ocean's Point Nemo, the spot on the planet farthest from land, at the right time in 2031, you'll get a good show, and the ocean will get a new permanent resident: the International Space Station (ISS). That's when the station's life will officially end, and it will come screaming through the atmosphere, slamming into the Pacific, never again to host astronauts or microgravity experiments or tension with mission control.

That crash will be aided by a SpaceX-built vehicle that will propel the ISS seaward with the aim of ensuring that its debris doesn't hit anyone or anything on the way down.

When a satellite takes a one-way trip through the atmosphere, the process is called *deorbiting*. That journey can be purposeful and controlled–as with the ISS. It can also be passive, in which a spacecraft is allowed to descend and burn up as it will. That latter option is the norm with small, new satellites and older satellites that are dead and out of anyone's control; sometimes, the latter are big enough that parts of them survive reentry.

In the coming years, the number of satellites set to launch–which will later have to deorbit–is due to increase drastically. Ensuring their lives end safely–minimizing risks to people, property, planes and the atmosphere itself–is no small task, whose details scientists, engineers and regulators are grappling with.

The biggest dangers come from larger spacecraft, old or new, that may not disintegrate on reentry. "A bunch of us have been calling for an end to uncontrolled reentries of massive satellites," says Jonathan McDowell, an astrophysicist at the Center for Astrophysics | Harvard & Smithsonian and publisher of the newsletter Jonathan's Space Report, which tracks space launches. "It's just not okay."

Deorbiting the space station is the most complicated get-out-of-space operation that will happen for the foreseeable future because the ISS is the largest humanmade structure that's ever been in space.

Because of its size, the station won't burn up completely in the atmosphere, as some smaller satellites do, but will instead scatter pieces the size of a microwave to the size of a car across whatever swath of the planet it crashes into.

To make sure that scattering happens over the empty Pacific and not, say, New York City, NASA has to push it there. And for that, the agency has hired SpaceX, which will build a special iteration of its Dragon spacecraft, the capsule that carries cargo and humans to and from the space station.

Called the U.S. Deorbit Vehicle (USDV), this Dragon will be more powerful than its ferrying cousins: it will have 46 thrusters instead of a mere 16, and it will boast a bigger trunk to house all those engines, six times the normal propellant and power systems that supply four times the usual juice. Once SpaceX is done building this steroidal Dragon, it will turn the $1.5-billion spacecraft over to NASA, which will own and operate it.

At the beginning of the operation, the USDV will dock to the ISS while the final crew is still there, so they can verify its working order. After that, NASA will let the station's orbit naturally decay, and the crew will depart when the station drops 70 kilometers lower than it is now. The spacecraft, as a ghost ship, will continue to downdraft for six months, naturally lowering to 220 kilometers above Earth. When the ISS is at the right point in its orbit, around two dozen of the special Dragon's thrusters will fire at once, sending it careening toward Point Nemo.

That fiery push may sound simple, but it's not, McDowell says. As the station dips lower into the atmosphere, the air gets thicker. "The winds are too much," he says, which "will make it hard to keep the station oriented." If the rocket scientists don't keep the station pointed in the right direction, they can't effectively use the thrusters to control its motion. "So you have to make the final engine burn from a high enough height that you've still got control over it," McDowell says.

And you have to boost its speed high enough and quick enough that it actually does deorbit and come down in the right place. It will be essential to achieve that oomph on the first try–likely why the USDV will have more engines than it necessarily needs. (SpaceX did not return a request for comment.)

The space station will be the flashiest thing that has ever returned from orbit. But it's far from the only thing that needs to come down. "You don't want to leave dead things in orbit, particularly low-Earth orbit, because it's very crowded," McDowell says. Also, big, dead objects will eventually reenter uncontrolled if left alone, putting a point in favor of planned deorbits. The Federal Communications Commission recently shortened the time gap allowed between when a low-orbiting satellite stops working and when it deorbits from 25 years to five years so that space traffic doesn't become unmanageable. But the U.S. isn't the only country with stuff in space, and the only international framework that exists is an unenforceable guideline from the Inter-Agency Space Debris Coordination Committee, which has stuck to the 25-year timeline. "It's very important to make sure that we keep the resource of space available for future generations," says Clare Martin, executive vice president of Astroscale US, a space sustainability company that works on technology to manage crowding in low Earth orbit.

With the new required U.S. timeline, and with so many satellites set to go to space as part of constellations like SpaceX's Starlink, the amount of material coming back down toward Earth is going to drastically increase. The descents of bigger satellites, such as the ISS, have to be controlled because pieces of them will survive the trip. But how big is big? "I think if it's under, say, half a ton, you probably don't need to worry," McDowell says. "If it's more than a few tons, you should worry. And in the middle, it sort of depends."

The stakes of deorbiting correctly are high because no one wants crowded orbits or, conversely, to be hit by space debris–which can happen and will only be statistically more likely in the future unless humans address their deorbiting issues. Parts of the trunks from Dragon spacecraft, for instance, have survived reentry to hit spots in North Carolina and Canada in 2024. Two pounds of debris survived from a pack of ISS batteries disposed of through the atmosphere, which then crashed through the roof of a Florida home.

Michael Kezirian, president of the International Space Safety Foundation and adjunct professor of astronautics practice at the University of Southern California, points to data on satellites that have fallen uncontrolled through the atmosphere. "About 30 percent of the mass survives, typically," he says. Larger components such as thrusters, pressure vessels, batteries and reaction wheels fail to fully incinerate.

If satellite operators want to make sure that mass doesn't come down on someone or something, they must actively control their spacecraft's reentry. That may involve hooking a satellite up to a powerful set of thrusters like the USDV's; smaller but similar systems could take out medium-sized spacecraft. Satellites can also use their own propellant and thrusters to complete their life in a planned way, or use special motors specifically meant for end-of-life maneuvers, like those made by space transportation company D-Orbit and installed before launch. Companies such as Airbus have worked on nets and harpoons that can wrap around or impale objects in space and bring them back down through the atmosphere.

Smaller satellites that will at least mostly burn up can also use some assistance in coming down in a timely but passive manner. Some companies have been working on tethers, essentially long metal strips that would fly behind satellites and convert their kinetic energy into electrical energy, slowing the satellite and sending it downward. There are also drag sails, thin material somewhat like a flat parachute that attaches to satellites to create more resistance with atmospheric particles and drag satellites down.

At Astroscale, Martin and her colleagues have done a demonstration mission called ELSA-d. For this mission, they attached a docking plate to a client's satellite and used their ELSA-d vehicle to magnetically capture that satellite and then release it. The follow-on ELSA-M mission will use similar technology to dock, release and deorbit actual spacecraft from the Internet services company Eutelsat OneWeb. "We have to take responsibility for what we're doing in orbit, and part of that is to use it to its advantage but then treat it responsibly afterwards and dispose of [our] stuff," Martin says, of satellite operators. "Move it out of the way."

Disposing of satellites involves tough choices. It isn't feasible for all the old spacecraft that went to orbit without a good plan for getting down to receive a good plan now.

Kezirian is concerned about the future of falling space debris from satellites old and new–including satellites that leave behind pieces that may not be lethal to anything on the ground but could be catastrophic for an airplane.

Kezirian has thought about this issue in relation to the Columbia shuttle disaster, when at least nine planes flew through the debris tail from the accident.

Those close calls resulted in NASA changing the shuttle landing procedures to better consider ground risks during an accident, and to improve collaboration between NASA and the Federal Aviation Administration in predicting and acting on potential debris.

Kezirian thinks more changes are in order. Right now sailors and pilots get notices from, for example, the Coast Guard and the FAA, respectively, about controlled deorbits. "Don't put your ship or plane in this area on Friday afternoon between 2 and 3 due to risks of falling space debris" is how McDowell summarizes these notices, which are called NOTAMs (Notices to Air Missions) for planes and LNMs (Local Notices to Mariners) for ships.

But not all space-debris events may result in such warnings. Although the chances of any one piece of space debris hitting any one plane are small, the more stuff you send sailing to Earth and the more air traffic you have, the higher the chances get–and the more likely you are to have a kind of black swan event in which a piece of a satellite's battery downs a plane of people.

According to Kezirian, officials need to get ahead of this problem before those chances rise too much as more and more satellites are launched. "You need to be much better at predicting the uncontrolled reentry," he says. "You have to have a very good idea of where the debris will be falling through the airspace. And then you need a way to provide timely notification to the pilot in command of an aircraft to move out of the way." These notices would be more like Waze for the skies than a NOTAM. Kezirian would like to extend the government's tight tracking of space debris down through the atmosphere and communicate that information to the air-navigation system, resulting in "dynamic closures of the airspace corresponding to the narrow footprint of reentering debris," allowing planes to effectively reroute.

Even if the issues with debris affecting flights and crashing through houses were solved, however, there would still be deorbiting problems caused by melting and vaporizing satellite ingredients, McDowell says. "You are changing the chemical composition of the upper atmosphere, as well as creating shockwaves in the upper atmosphere that themselves have chemistry effects," he says.

Experts are beginning to be concerned that that effect might actually be substantial and that it will grow more so. In samples of the rarefied air, "there's all of this sort of metallic crap there that didn't used to be there that looks like it's from vaporized spacecraft," McDowell says. He's currently working on a paper estimating how much of that foreign material remains in the atmosphere. "We just don't know yet what the effects are," he says. "But that doesn't mean you go, 'Oh, well, no worries,' right?"

Deorbiting, it turns out, is *mostly* worries. And determining how to assuage them, scientifically and technologically, will be key to ensuring both space and Earth stay safe. "We need to keep addressing this problem now. We can't wait and hope it will go away," Martin says. "It won't."

About the Author

Sarah Scoles is a Colorado-based science journalist and a contributing editor at Scientific American. *Her newest book is* Countdown: The Blinding Future of Nuclear Weapons *(Bold Type Books, 2024).*

What the Amazon versus SpaceX Satellite Mega Constellation War Means for Earth

By Jonathan O'Callaghan

Humanity's aspirations have long pushed the boundaries of our delicate balance with nature, from our expanding industrial might to our prowling of the seas. For the past several years, our ambitions have spread in earnest to the heavens, threatening to pollute space itself in a manner never seen before. Now a fresh batch of hardware that is making its way to orbit–a stack of two dozen satellites from delivery giant Amazon that are designed to send the Internet to Earth from space–highlights once again the challenges facing our civilization. While sating the needs of a growing technological populace on the ground, large satellite constellations such as Amazon's risk a fundamental alteration of the appearance, and usability, of the night sky–and we still don't have solutions.

On April 28 at 7:01 p.m. EDT, an Atlas V rocket lifted off from Cape Canaveral, Fla. Onboard, it carried the first 27 satellites of a planned 3,200 from Amazon, founded by Jeff Bezos: the start of a grand new satellite collection–often referred to as a mega constellation–known as Project Kuiper. The goal of these satellites, now making their way to orbit, is to beam Internet to users in remote locations away from terrestrial infrastructure, such as in rural areas or on planes.

But Amazon is not alone. SpaceX, under its CEO Elon Musk, has already launched more than 7,000 flat, car-width satellites in its Starlink constellation and plans to add some 30,000 more. The company boasts more than 5 million customers around the globe, with monthly subscription costs for residential plans ranging from $80 to $120 in the U.S. Users also need to fork out $349 for a dish to connect to the satellites, which then provides a Wi-Fi network for them to connect to. That equates to revenues of hundreds of millions of dollars a month, with the potential for billions of dollars as the service expands and the number of users increases. And it is a slice of this pie that Amazon is hoping to grab.

Reports suggest Project Kuiper might cost Amazon as much as $20 billion to build. "Amazon wouldn't be investing the best part of $20 billion unless they perceived a multibillion-dollar opportunity," says Tim Farrar, a satellite communications expert in California. Indeed, Amazon's CEO Andy Jassy has previously spoken about Project Kuiper becoming the company's "fourth pillar" alongside its online marketplace, Web cloud services and Amazon Prime subscriptions.

To compete with Starlink, Amazon plans to launch fast. The company has bought space on dozens of rockets–including SpaceX's own Falcon 9–to rapidly get its hardware into space. The need for speed is not only because of SpaceX: as part of Amazon's license with the Federal Communications Commission (FCC) to operate its satellites in space, the company must launch half of its planned constellation of 3,200 satellites by July 2026 and the remaining satellites by July 2029 to retain that license.

Starlink has dramatically changed the environment around Earth. When the first Starlink satellites were launched in May 2019, there were barely 2,000 active satellites in space. Today there are more than 11,000. Most of these are Starlink satellites, but the figure also includes 648 satellites that provide the European-based company Eutelsat's OneWeb space Internet service and 72 satellites from a growing Chinese space Internet constellation called Qianfan, which may eventually reach 14,000. This rapidly increasing number of satellites raises concerns about how we manage all of these objects. "Every day is unprecedented territory," says Hugh Lewis, a space debris expert at the University of Southampton in England.

Project Kuiper is designed to orbit slightly above Starlink, at an altitude of about 370 to 390 miles (590 to 630 kilometers), compared with Starlink's 340 miles (550 km). Both constellations' satellites are designed to be constantly replenished as they fail or reach the end of their life, with SpaceX currently launching Starlink satellites in batches of dozens multiple times a month. That means there will constantly be Kuiper satellites crossing over with Starlink satellites as they travel up and down, with significant potential for chaos.

All of the satellites in the current Starlink constellation combined perform about 50,000 collision avoidance maneuvers every six months, according to SpaceX. In these cases, a Starlink satellite is deemed to pass close enough to another object in orbit that a collision could be possible, prompting the satellite to perform an automated navigation away from the object using its thrusters. Amazon has not yet announced its own automated system, and neither that company nor SpaceX responded to a request for comment from *Scientific American*. Nevertheless, with the introduction of Project Kuiper and other mega constellations, the number of close approaches across all satellites could grow to the "tens or even hundreds of millions" per year, Lewis says. "Ultimately we're going to be bitten by one of those."

The collision of two satellites would be a disaster. In 2009 the U.S. Iridium 33 satellite collided with the defunct Russian satellite Kosmos 2251, producing thousands of pieces of debris, some of which will orbit Earth for 100 years. The biggest danger of another collision is that the resultant debris could cause further collisions as more and more satellites are hit. "It's not going to be like *WALL·E*," says Victoria Samson, chief director of space security and stability at the Secure World Foundation, a space sustainability nonprofit organization, referring to a 2008 Pixar film in which a future Earth has been encompassed by space junk. "But at a certain point, it is going to be extremely complicated to operate in low-Earth orbit." And regardless of the potential for collisions, the huge bulk of satellites going up must also come back down at some point and reenter our atmosphere, which might be depleting ozone.

Efforts to introduce regulation to oversee this rapid growth in satellites has been slow going. No formal international laws or bodies currently exist to monitor or control the number of satellites in orbit. We are "not at all" ready for the arrival of so many satellites, says Michelle Hanlon, a space lawyer at the

University of Mississippi. "We can't agree on anything in the international community. We ought to have a space corridor or space arbitration so at least we get all of the space issues in one jurisdiction. We don't have anything." Eventually "there's going to be a breaking point," she says—and an actual collision may be necessary to spur meaningful action.

And then there is the astronomy issue. For years, astronomers have been grappling with Starlink's effect on their observations of the universe. The mega constellation's numerous satellites appear as constant bright streaks in images from telescopes on Earth and even some in space. Samantha Lawler, an astronomer at the University of Regina in Saskatchewan, says that many of her images are marred by satellites crossing her plane of view. "I find it horrifying," she says. "All of the downsides are coming to pass, and there's still no regulation."

Bright satellite streaks can hinder scientific discovery because they sometimes obscure interesting objects of study behind them such as asteroids, planets and stars. They can also alter the natural aesthetic of the night sky. "One of the main recommendations of the IAU [International Astronomical Union] is to keep the satellites under [a brightness of] magnitude 7," says Olivier Hainaut, an astronomer at the European Southern Observatory in Germany. "That means you don't see them with the naked eye." One telescope that might be particularly affected is the Vera C. Rubin Observatory, a new telescope built in the mountains of Chile with a huge camera that will image the entire sky once every three days starting later this year. But satellite trails could affect a third of its images, significantly hampering its science.

SpaceX has been moderately successful at dimming Starlink satellites by applying a darkened coating or using a sunshade to lower the amount of sunlight they reflect to the ground, but other satellites such as those in China's Qianfan constellation are even brighter. "Those ones are very worrying," Lawler says. And even radio astronomy can be affected by incoming satellite signals. The problems for astronomers are mounting, with no obvious solution in sight. "Five years ago we were living in blissful ignorance," Hainaut says.

The Kuiper satellites' ultimate brightness won't be clear until a few weeks after this first launch, when they will have been raised to their operational altitude. By then we might have already seen the next Kuiper launch, followed by the next and the next. Providing widespread Internet from space in our modern digital world is a worthy goal that can benefit many people on the planet. But as our cosmic infrastructure grows without any clear rules of the road, so, too, does the potential for disaster. "At some point, we have to stop launching these constellations," Hanlon says, either until those rules become clear or the worst does happen, and two satellites collide. "I hope we figure it out."

About the Author

Jonathan O'Callaghan is an award-winning freelance journalist covering astronomy, astrophysics, commercial spaceflight and space exploration. Follow him on X @ Astro_Jonny

Why We Need to Reduce, Reuse and Recycle in Space

By Moriba Jah

A decade ago humanity launched around 200 objects into space per year. Now we launch more than 2,600, with no prospects for slowing down. This rapid expansion of human activity in outer space has filled Earth orbit with space trash, from dead satellites to used-up rocket parts. The region is already so crowded that working satellites run the risk of colliding with bits of garbage from previous generations of spacecraft. Even the International Space Station often has to adjust its orbit to dodge debris.

Currently there are more than 25,000 pieces of trackable human-made junk larger than 10 centimeters orbiting Earth. The more we put up there, the greater the chance that pieces of debris (traveling at relative speeds up to 15 times faster than a bullet) will strike working spacecraft, creating even more dangerous trash. The catastrophic collision in 2009 between the defunct Russian satellite Cosmos 2251 and the operational Iridium satellite, for example, generated nearly 2,000 debris fragments, many of which are still being tracked today.

Orbital space is a finite resource, and it's rapidly being consumed by a few organizations, notably SpaceX, OneWeb and Amazon's Project Kuiper. SpaceX, for instance, owns and operates the majority of all working satellites, and the company aims to launch tens of thousands more satellites to provide global broadband Internet coverage. Similarly, Amazon plans to deploy 3,236 satellites for its broadband network.

Giving everyone unfettered access without global coordination and planning means that eventually no one may be able to use it.

If we keep up this pace, orbital space will become unusable—especially the most popular region, low Earth orbit (LEO), which extends up to 2,000 kilometers in altitude. When looking at all orbital regions, we may lose services we've come to rely on: continuous communications, GPS mapping, Internet, Earth monitoring, and more. Today nearly every satellite that is launched is equivalent to a piece of single-use plastic, in that its fate is to become detritus. We are heading toward a tragedy of the commons in orbital space: giving everyone unfettered access without global coordination and planning means that eventually no one may be able to use it.

As we continue to push the boundaries of space exploration and commercialization, there is a growing movement to rethink our approach to using the space environment–to move to a strategy anchored in stewardship and sound waste-management principles. I believe we must leave behind our "linear space economy," where we use and abandon, and move toward a "circular space economy"–a sustainable way to use space that emphasizes the reuse, recycling, and efficient management of space resources.

Just as we are reckoning with how to conserve ecosystems on Earth for future living creatures, we must think of space as an environment worthy of preservation. In fact, reforming how we operate in space is critical for Earth conservation.

The production, launch and operation of satellites and rockets consume vast amounts of resources and energy, contributing to greenhouse gas emissions and environmental degradation. Rocket launches release pollutants into the atmosphere, including carbon dioxide, soot and aluminum oxides, which cause atmospheric damage and contribute to climate change.

Moreover, the practice of uncontrolled reentries, where defunct satellites and rocket stages are allowed to burn up in the atmosphere, adds to atmospheric pollution and creates the risk of debris falling on people and property on Earth. In 2024, for instance, pieces of a SpaceX Dragon service module, including one about the size of a standard car hood, landed in the mountains of North Carolina, and a castoff part of the International Space Station fell through the roof of a house in Naples, Fla.

A circular space economy would represent a paradigm shift toward sustainable space practices, drawing inspiration from circular economy ideas that are gaining traction here on Earth. “Circularity” in this sense refers to waste-management principles calling for the end of life of a product to be designed for the object’s reuse or recycling. The first step is to design spacecraft using materials that minimize pollution and generate less waste. The second is to repair satellites’ broken parts in orbit to extend their life cycles. The third is to recycle materials from defunct satellites for use on new missions, without having to bring the satellites back to Earth. And finally, we must retrieve and reprocess space debris to reduce collision risks and reclaim valuable components.

We won’t be able to enact a circular space economy without some technological innovations. We don’t currently have techniques to service all spacecraft in orbit, although several companies and space agencies are working on it. We must create technology to extend satellites’ operational lifespans and reduce the need for costly and resource-intensive replacement missions. We need spacecraft that can approach aging satellites and dock with them, using robots to repair, refuel and upgrade them.

Space exploration also raises fundamental ethical questions about fair resource extraction, ownership and environmental stewardship.

We’ll also need a way to reuse and recycle satellites when their working lives are over. Currently all satellites become trash when their primary mission ends, and new satellites are built from entirely new materials. It’s a huge waste, much like our junkyards for used cars and other vehicles. Researchers are working on ways to harvest materials from dead spacecraft to integrate into new vehicles and to use techniques to build new satellites out of used parts.

A positive step in this direction is the reusable rocket technology SpaceX is developing. The boosters of their Falcon 9 rockets, for instance, can land vertically after being jettisoned in space after launch, allowing them to fly again. Not only does this save money–recycling boosters reduces the cost of each Falcon 9 launch by up to 30 percent–it generates less trash. But so far SpaceX is the only company or agency launching satellites with reusable rockets. We need more.

There's also been movement toward servicing working satellites in orbit. Northrop Grumman's SpaceLogistics has developed a spacecraft, the Mission Extension Vehicle (MEV), to help aging satellites keep going. In 2020 it successfully docked with the Intelsat 901 satellite, which was running out of fuel, and began using its own thrusters and propellant to maneuver the joined craft, extending the Intelsat's operational life. A second MEV docked with another Intelsat spacecraft in 2021. When those satellites are ready to be retired, the MEVs can undock and move on to other spacecraft that need their help. Launching an MEV to aid an ailing craft costs about half to a quarter of the price of building and launching an entirely new satellite. In addition to saving money, in-orbit servicing reduces the frequency of new satellite launches, which in turn minimizes the accumulation of space debris and the greenhouse gas emissions that come with rocket launches.

Removing debris from orbit is another challenge. Different types of trash require different removal techniques, with many ideas coming from the fishing industry: some strategies use nets, others harpoons, and still others hooks. Each removal technology has limitations and works only for a subset of the objects that need to be fished out of orbital space. It's also really expensive to retrieve any kind of space trash because anything that is not being actively controlled in space is tumbling. This means that to grab something to remove it, you must either find a way to steady the space detritus or make your debris-removal satellite tumble along with it. Detumbling debris takes a lot of energy, which results in high propellant costs.

Nevertheless, some progress has been made. In 2021 a Tokyo-based company, Astroscale, ran the End-of-Life Services by Astroscale demonstration (ELSA-d) mission, which launched two satellites: one to simulate a dead spacecraft and a servicer satellite to remove it. The two craft successfully docked in orbit and then released, testing out a critical process for eventual debris removal. The company plans to run more tests with its Active Debris Removal by Astroscale-Japan (ADRAS-J) mission, which launched in 2024.

The European Space Agency (ESA), partnering with start-up ClearSpace, is set to launch its ClearSpace-1 mission in 2028. ClearSpace-1 will use four robotic arms to grab onto the agency's PROBA-1 satellite and bring it safely out of orbit. The project aims not only to clean up space but also to develop the ability to target larger and more complex pieces of debris.

Finally, more efficient propulsion technology allows spacecraft to use less fuel and last longer on their initial load. Electric propulsion systems, such as ion thrusters and Hall effect thrusters, are newer technologies that offer higher efficiency and fuel economy compared with traditional chemical propulsion. These systems use electric power to ionize propellant and generate thrust, enabling spacecraft to achieve higher velocities and perform precise maneuvers over extended periods. Electric propulsion is already used by many working satellites and will become increasingly common.

As we design new technology to conserve space, we'd do well to take inspiration from another kind of tech: Indigenous societies' traditional ecological knowledge (TEK). This kind of TEK emphasizes the importance of harmonious relationships between human activities and the environment. It shows us that we have to see space as an extension of our natural world, where resources must be managed wisely and responsibly.

An example of applying TEK ideas to modern space activities is a recent collaboration between the ESA and Indigenous groups in Australia to study the impacts of space debris on wildlife habitats. By respecting the wisdom of Indigenous communities, ESA not only advanced their scientific goals but also promoted a sustainable model that can be applied to future space missions.

New technology alone isn't enough to fix the space junk problem—we'll need legal reform, too. The current global space policy is a patchwork of regulations that often lag behind technological advancements and the evolving needs of space activities. SpaceX, for instance, has faced regulatory challenges in deploying its reusable rockets because our laws haven't caught up with the technology. Fragmented regulations across different countries and regions also lead to inconsistencies and hinder international collaboration. And many existing space policies don't even address sustainable practices such as in-orbit servicing, space debris mitigation and responsible resource use.

The European Union is trying to pave the way by integrating sustainability principles into its space policies. The E.U. has streamlined licensing processes for satellite launches and in-orbit operations across member states and has allocated significant funding for research and development on dealing with space debris. The U.S., through its many government agencies, has begun working to streamline the licensing process as well. But most countries are dangerously far behind.

Governments have a strong hand to play in incentivizing companies to design and develop sustainable space systems. One way to do this would be to adopt what are called extended producer responsibility laws, which require companies to help manage the waste from the technology they produce. Perhaps governments could use a credit system to regulate the amount of space debris the industry is allowed to create. Laws could also incentivize the design, launch and operation of on-orbit recycling centers where aging and defunct satellites could be repurposed.

Ultimately the governments that permit spacecraft to be launched are liable for any damage their space objects may cause. So the responsibility for cleaning orbital space falls to governments, but none of them, including Russia, the U.S. or China, are establishing robust markets for space garbage pickup and removal services. Moreover, currently there is no legal mechanism to transfer this liability for damage from one launching state to another, making it complicated to put in place a space salvage law analogous to maritime policy. The United Nations Committee on the Peaceful Uses of Outer Space also plays a pivotal role in developing international space law and norms. Its Space Debris Mitigation Guidelines encourage member states to manage space debris and promote sustainable space operations. More than 100 countries have endorsed the guidelines, including the U.S. Yet guidelines are not enforceable laws in and of themselves—they are merely suggestions.

Space exploration also raises fundamental ethical questions about fair resource extraction, ownership and environmental stewardship. Asteroid mining, for example, presents opportunities for accessing rare minerals and resources, although it also risks destroying the scientific and cultural heritage of celestial bodies. And space mining could destabilize global markets—imagine mining an asteroid made out of platinum. Furthermore, who should be allowed to profit from the resources of asteroids—is it fair for only certain countries, or certain billionaires, to grow even richer and more powerful from space commodities?

Organizations such as the International Institute of Space Law and the U.N. Office for Outer Space Affairs are trying to develop ethical guidelines for responsible ways to use space resources that emphasize transparency, international cooperation and sustainability. Initiatives such as the Space Sustainability Rating, which aims to certify space missions based on sustainable practices, could encourage companies and nations to act responsibly.

Preserving the space environment for future generations is a moral imperative. In the short term, we must take immediate action to deal with the growing dangers of space junk. We need more funding for debris-tracking and debris-mitigation technologies. We must also start changing how we build and use satellites to waste fewer resources, produce less trash and pollution, and recycle more. A circular space economy is the only way to keep space usable indefinitely.

In the long term, fostering international cooperation—and international treaties requiring sustainable space practices—is critical. The Inter-Agency Space Debris Coordination Committee, an intergovernmental organization dedicated to combating the problem of orbital trash, is a promising step. Many space agencies, including NASA, China's National Space Administration and Roscosmos, are members. The ESA's Clean Space initiative is another smart approach to reducing space debris through technology development and policy changes.

The establishment of a circular space economy is not just an option but a necessity for the sustainable future of space exploration. By adopting the principles of reuse, recycling, and efficient resource management, we can lower the risks of space debris collisions, preserve resources, and ensure that outer space remains a viable domain for scientific discovery and commercial innovation. Policymakers, industry leaders, scientists and the global community must embrace a sustainable approach to our activities in Earth orbit, securing its potential for generations to come.

About the Author

Moriba Jah is a celestial steward and space environmentalist. He is a professor of aerospace engineering at the University of Texas at Austin, as well as co-founder and chief scientist of space sustainability start-up Privateer and decision intelligence company GaiaVerse. His work focuses on the sustainable use of outer space, the development of innovative solutions to space debris, and providing decision intelligence to solve other environmental challenges.

Scientists Race to Map Dangerous Ultrasmall Space Junk

By Sharmila Kuthunur

Imagine a world in which workers providing crucial services such as weather forecasting and global broadband Internet had to do their jobs while dodging bullets on an active shooting range. At the very least, you'd probably worry about their well-being, right?

This isn't actually a make-believe scenario: the world we're imagining is our own, the shooting range is Earth's orbit, and the at-risk "workers" are satellites there (as well as crewed vehicles and habitats) threatened by skyrocketing amounts of space junk. Nearly 70 years have passed since the onset of the space age with the launch of Sputnik 1, the first artificial satellite. And in that time, the heavens above have become cluttered with thousands of spent rocket bodies, dead spacecraft and sizable pieces of hardware, all circling our planet at dangerously high speeds.

The U.S. Air Force monitors roughly 25,000 pieces of trash in low-Earth orbit (LEO), the busiest and most crowded region, which encompasses orbits of 2,000 kilometers or less in altitude. Current telescopes and radar technology limit the smallest trackable pieces to approximately 10 centimeters across, about the size of a bagel. Everything else–and there's quite a lot of it, mostly in the form of millions of paint flecks and bits of spacecraft–is too small to be presently cataloged but can still pose extreme hazards. This so-called lethal nontrackable debris can travel around Earth at speeds of about 10 kilometers per second, or more than 22,000 miles per hour, meaning that even an otherwise-unnoticeable speck will pack a potent wallop. Indeed, in 2016, when a millimeter-sized piece of debris struck a solar panel of the European Space Agency (ESA) satellite Sentinel-1A, the impact was so strong that it punched a 40-centimeter hole in the panel and tilted the satellite askew. The risk to humans isn't negligible either. Mere weeks ago a decommissioned

Russian satellite broke into more than 100 large fragments that prompted astronauts on the International Space Station to take shelter, an incident that may have been the result of a collision with a similar uncataloged piece of debris.

"There's a lot of them. They're not tracked. And they're dangerous," says astrophysicist Jonathan C. McDowell regarding the tiny pieces of space junk. "At orbital velocities, even quite a small object is really gonna smack you."

Without a clear way for anyone to see all that tiny debris, it's impossible to alert satellite operators of imminent, potentially catastrophic collisions–let alone to know the true scale of the threat.

But that may soon change. The U.S. government is now trying to develop a real-time monitoring capability for the millions of ultrasmall pieces of space junk–that is, from 10 centimeters down to a millimeter in size–throughout low-Earth orbit and even beyond. Called the Space Debris Identification and Tracking (SINTRA) program, the effort involves more than 100 scientists across a dozen institutions. As a key first step, SINTRA is leveraging supercomputers and artificial intelligence algorithms trained on extensive archival data to detect the telltale signatures created by tiny, fast-moving debris. Examples include fleeting bursts of light sparked when two pieces of junk collide and faint, wavelike plasma wakes in Earth's electrically charged upper atmosphere made by debris streaking through, both of which scientists suspect can be used to help track and study the hazardous flotsam.

To support that work, researchers at the Naval Research Laboratory (NRL) in Washington, D.C., will soon seek to replicate some of these effects by accelerating fragments of common satellite materials such as aluminum, silicon and aerospace-grade plastic to hypervelocity speeds inside a large vacuum chamber. The results–including specific frequencies at which the lightninglike bursts occur, the amount of time they last and the rate at which clouds of dust form and expand in the aftermath of collisions–can then be used to better train the algorithms. This will ensure the team can unearth more of the myriad past collisions that were inadvertently recorded in the archives. And the eventual outcome could be a massive daily operation to track minuscule debris by the millions and create a new early-warning system for possible collisions with working satellites.

"It's a reflection of how both our challenges and our capabilities have grown that one can think of doing this," says McDowell, who is not involved with the SINTRA program. "It's a lot of work to go to the next order of magnitude in space tracking, but it has to be done."

As part of a broader, government-wide effort to address space debris risks, SINTRA was officially launched last August by the Intelligence Advanced Research Projects Activity (IARPA), a federal organization that sponsors research projects to benefit the country's intelligence community. "We're trying to revolutionize how we're looking at the problem," says Alexis Truitt of IARPA, who leads the program. "SINTRA sits really well within that vision."

She declined to specify the project's cost but said driving the state-of-the-art effort "requires significant investment." A publicly available Q&A about the program notes IARPA has historically budgeted its projects between $50 million and $100 million, with contracts for individual teams typically capped at $25 million. "At IARPA, we follow a high-risk, high-payoff model," Truitt says, "in that we will take on considerable risk to solve hard research problems that may be too risky for our government partners to pursue otherwise."

Tracking the Nontrackable

The outsize energies associated with even minuscule space debris smashups could prove crucial to gaining a better overall view of just how much junk is actually whirling around Earth.

Previous research has shown that when two specks of material collide at very high speed, they crumble into a cloud of charged gas and tiny fragments that creates intense bursts of light–a bit like micro thunderbolts–as it expands. The charged fragments can also generate electric pulses when they brush past each other. These emissions are strong enough to be picked up by instruments on Earth, such as radio antennas in NASA's Deep Space Network, according to recent simulations conducted by a team at the University of Michigan as part of the SINTRA project. Following the hypervelocity experiments at NRL and subsequent algorithmic training of debris-scouting AIs, the researchers hope to spot as many as 100 small-scale collisions in space every day.

"It's never been done before," says Mojtaba Akhavan-Tafti of the University of Michigan, a member of the team that conducted the recent simulations and a scientist on the SINTRA project. "This is a new field being created by this research, so you don't have colleagues that have done this for many years to go and ask questions to."

Similarly, scientists at SRI International, a nonprofit research institute headquartered in California, are training ground-based radars and other instruments to detect the tenuous wakes rippling through our planet's upper atmosphere that are caused by impinging orbital debris. Finding and following these trails should allow observers to identify and localize the corresponding pieces of junk. The same team also plans to run a test using a large radio telescope at Stanford University, nicknamed the Dish, to see whether the researchers can use radar signals to map more of the tiny orbital debris.

"We are tackling some very hard problems," Truitt says. "The debris problem is bigger than one entity could handle, so [SINTRA] is just a piece of the bigger puzzle."

Another puzzle piece that SINTRA personnel are pondering is how to handle the drastic spike in collision alerts expected from continuously tracking millions of debris objects. Satellite operators are typically notified of worrisome possible collisions a week in advance by the 18th Space Defense Squadron of the U.S. Space Force, which monitors known orbiting debris through its Space Surveillance Network. But because of the significant fuel costs for maneuvering and uncertainties from the highly dynamic orbital environment, decisions to dodge "are taken as late as possible," usually in the final 24 hours, says Francesca Litizia, a space debris mitigation engineer at the ESA. But data that are paramount for those decisions –such as whether the objects on a potential collision course can be maneuvered and, if so, which party should swerve–are not often available or up-to-date. "Now we still have to call [satellite operators] on the phone and hope that someone replies on the other side," says Litizia, who is not directly involved in the SINTRA program. "Of course, this is not very scalable in the future."

"We would need to revolutionize how we provide alerts to our satellite operators," Truitt acknowledges.

Too Much Orbital Trash

"We think that space is very large, but we ignore the fact that humans are also very good at trashing the environment," Akhavan-Tafti says. That so much orbital trash has accumulated in less than seven decades of space activities–the blink of an eye compared with Earth's 4.5-billion-year history–is indeed alarming. Astronomer Aaron C. Boley, who studies orbital debris as co-director of the Outer Space Institute, hopes SINTRA will create "a greater sense of awareness of what's been done so that we can be much more careful about the way we are using low-Earth orbit."

Multiple recent milestones offer hope for improvement. Chief among them is the 2022 ruling by the U.S. Federal Communications Commission (FCC) that shortened the period of time defunct satellites were allowed to stay in orbit according to a long-standing guideline from 25 to five years. Last year ESA followed suit with the Zero Debris Charter, a set of guidelines for its 22 member countries and the global space community to follow to become debris-neutral by 2030. India, too, has vowed to achieve debris-free missions by the end of the decade. Many scientists hope other spacefaring nations will soon apply similar practices to their own space assets. "It's very important that these sorts of regulations exist so that everyone can benefit from the space environment," Akhavan-Tafti says.

Any effort to clean up our orbital trash would begin with determining where the objects are, so SINTRA and other debris-detection programs seem destined to become essential enablers of future space activity. It is equally important, however, to address the fundamental problem–the thousands of large derelict spacecraft and rocket stages that created most of the smaller debris in the first place, Boley says. "That's gonna be hard," he adds. "These things are the size of school buses and are spinning rapidly."

Multiple commercial debris removal services are nonetheless eager to rise to the challenge. Noteworthy among them is Astroscale, a start-up headquartered in Tokyo that was recently commissioned by the Japanese government to demonstrate its abilities by rendezvousing with and removing a defunct rocket stage from orbit. Looking ahead, in 2026 a Switzerland-based start-up named ClearSpace is scheduled to launch an ESA-funded mission to meet up with and deorbit a hefty hunk of space debris as well.

Even if such approaches prove wildly effective, Boley, Akhavan-Tafti and other scientists interviewed for this story all share a common concern: Can any effort to take out Earth's orbital trash counteract the all-too-human tendency to maintain the status quo, treating the sky itself as a dumping ground? The lessons from history are discouraging; domains long considered too big and remote to be subject to human foibles are increasingly disrupted by them. The plastic in our oceans, pollution in our air and clear-cut wastes where forests once stood all offer mute testament to our hubris. Now something similar is unfolding again in the heavens above, and we are only beginning to grasp the implications.

"My worry is how we just continuously do this and don't seem to learn," Boley says. "We still have the opportunity to do something before there is a tragedy."

About the Author

Sharmila Kuthunur is an independent space journalist based in Bengaluru, India. Her work has also appeared in Science, Space.com, Astronomy and Live Science, among other publications. She has earned a master's degree in journalism from Northeastern University in Boston. Follow her on BlueSky: @skuthunur.bsky.social

Section 2: Space Missions and Stations

If SpaceX Goes Public in 2026, What Does That Mean for Space Exploration?

By Ramin Skibba

Elon Musk's SpaceX may be on the cusp of going public: The company, which almost went bankrupt in the 2000s, is mulling an initial public offering (IPO) that would value it at as much as $1.5 trillion. The move could raise tens of billions of dollars for SpaceX, but there's more than money at stake–the future of space exploration hangs in the balance, too.

SpaceX is integral to numerous critical missions with both NASA and the Pentagon, including ferrying crew and cargo to the International Space Station, placing satellites in orbit and being key to NASA's plan to return astronauts to the moon by 2028. Its Starlink satellite Internet service is booming. And lest we forget, the company has its own long-term vision to land on and even colonize Mars.

Going public would put SpaceX in the company of older, traditional aerospace heavyweights, such as Boeing and Northrop Grumman, and industry upstarts, such as Rocket Lab and Firefly Aerospace. Still, SpaceX's plans are startling, experts say.

"The fact that it's maybe an all-in, holistic SpaceX IPO is a bit of a surprise," says Matthew Weinzierl, a Harvard Business School researcher, who studies the private space sector. There was a sense that Musk might take Starlink, a subsidiary of SpaceX, public because it makes so much money but not that he would do so with the whole company, Weinzierl says.

If SpaceX goes public, that will mean more scrutiny, more shareholder interest and–perhaps most critically for space science–more investment to bolster its research and development work. "SpaceX has been a major driver of a lot of what we're seeing in outer space right now," both positive and negative, says Aaron Boley, a planetary scientist at the University of British Columbia and co-founder of the Outer Space Institute, a network of space experts.

An IPO could bring in an influx of capital to fund new projects, Weinzierl says, such as building solar-powered, orbital data centers to support artificial intelligence, perhaps including that of Musk's own AI company xAI. Musk had suggested as much in October.

Fresh money could also support SpaceX in its work with NASA and the U.S. Department of Defense. The company's contracts include billions of dollars to transport NASA astronauts and cargo to and from space, a $255-million deal to launch NASA's Nancy Grace Roman Space Telescope in the spring of 2027 and billions of dollars to loft defense satellites into Earth orbit as part of the National Security Space Launch program. And in late October, the *Wall Street Journal* reported that SpaceX was set to secure a $2-billion contract to work on President Donald Trump's Golden Dome missile defense project, for which it would develop satellites to track missiles and aircraft.

Considering that NASA and the Pentagon are already so reliant on the commercial space industry–and especially SpaceX–going public might not change the company's relationship with either agency much, says Clayton Swope, deputy director of the Aerospace Security Project at the Center for Strategic & International Studies, a Washington, D.C.–based think tank. And SpaceX may have another government ally in recently confirmed NASA administrator Jared Isaacman. He flew to space with Space on two missions: *Inspiration4* and *Polaris Dawn*.

SpaceX's potential IPO comes at a moment of grave uncertainty for NASA. Doubt is swirling around the future of the agency's Artemis moon program, which is supposed to land astronauts on the lunar surface in 2028. SpaceX nabbed the NASA contract to build and operate its Human Landing System using SpaceX's Starship megarocket as part of the *Artemis III* and *Artemis IV* missions. (Jeff Bezos's rival company, Blue Origin, received the contract for *Artemis V*.)

Yet *Artemis III*–slated to be the first time astronauts will set foot on the moon since *Apollo 17* in 1972–has been delayed numerous times, in part because of problems with SpaceX's still-in-development Starship. To support Artemis, SpaceX plans to launch multiple Starships that would be able to refuel while in orbit and to send a modified Starship lander to the lunar surface. But the company has yet to show that the rocket is capable of any of that. Now SpaceX is in danger of losing the contract altogether: citing rising competition with China, U.S. secretary of transportation Sean Duffy, then acting chief of NASA, reopened competition for the *Artemis III* contract in October.

What all this means for would-be investors is that buying a stake in SpaceX comes with risks, especially considering the multiple mishaps the company has faced with Starship–not to mention Musk's own controversial politics and business practices.

"If you're buying into an IPO for SpaceX, then you're buying into the way they do business, which has explosive failures as well as spectacular successes," Swope says. Still, while SpaceX's visions for the moon and Mars may or may not come to pass, the company continues to attract top-tier talent in addition to investor interest.

A publicly traded SpaceX would also mean that shareholders would have a voice in the company's decisions, which could create tension with Musk, who is "not fond" of checks on his authority, according to Wendy Whitman Cobb, a professor of strategy and security studies at the School of Advanced Air and Space Studies at Air University. Planetary scientist Boley hopes shareholders would hold SpaceX to account regarding its environmental and security record: the company has numerous "dual-use" spacecraft that serve both civilian and military customers. And with nearly 10,000 Starlink satellites in orbit, its risk of collisions–and potential debris raining down on Earth–is also growing.

Ultimately, it remains to be seen if Musk and SpaceX's leadership will go through with an IPO.

"Things seem to change fast in D.C. and the space community. It might not be a done deal," Swope says.

About the Author

Ramin Skibba is a science writer based in San Diego, Calif. He can be found at https://raminskibba.net

Why More Space Launches Could Be a Good Thing for the Climate

By Riis Williams

The weather was mild on the evening of May 25 at the southern tip of the Māhia Peninsula in New Zealand. The wind was gentle, the sky was clear, and even conditions in the Earth's upper atmosphere were calm. It was, in every way, a promising night for a rocket launch. And at 7:41 P.M. local time that promise was fulfilled when an Electron booster from the space technology company Rocket Lab lifted off from the company's launch site and carried a shoebox-sized infrared NASA satellite into a near-polar orbit around Earth.

The Electron launch was the first of two that Rocket Lab completed within less than two weeks for NASA's Polar Radiant Energy in the Far-InfraRed Experiment (PREFIRE), a 10-month mission to measure how much heat emanates into space from Antarctica and the Arctic. The satellites' data will help inform models projecting the magnitude of one of climate change's most frightening effects—the melting of polar ice sheets and the resulting sea-level rise. The mission, like Rocket Lab itself, is meant to punch well above its weight and is emblematic of the company's plans for blending high-impact science with efficient and accessible space travel and manufacturing, says Rocket Lab's founder and chief executive officer Peter Beck.

Rockets and space travel are carbon-intensive: a single launch can emit hundreds of tons of greenhouse gases. But Beck says that shouldn't preclude space companies acting sustainably and serving worthy climate causes—while also expanding access to low-Earth orbit and beyond. Rocket Lab's Electron, for example, is the only small orbital launch vehicle in the world that is designed to be largely reusable. It is equipped with a parachute system that carries the booster's engine-packed bottom stage back down to Earth. The mechanism is still being tested, but the hope, Beck says, is that Electron's reusability will limit its waste and keep its launches relatively cheap, making space-based research more affordable for smaller organizations and educational institutions.*

During a conversation with *Scientific American*, Beck discussed PREFIRE and how Rocket Lab and other companies can responsibly navigate the increasingly competitive commercial space industry and support climate science.

[*An edited transcript of the interview follows.*]

Rocket Lab describes itself as an end-to-end company. What does this mean in the aerospace industry?

End-to-end means that we have the capacity to design the satellite and all its components; build it, test it, then launch it on one of our own rockets; and, once it's finally in orbit, operate it for an organization or other commercial entity down here on Earth. Sometimes we even get to design the satellite's mission. We're basically running everything from one end of the spectrum to the other. Typically the space industry is bifurcated into "launch" and "satellites," and there are few companies in the world–or even in the history of the space industry–with the capability to do both. For PREFIRE specifically, our job is only to launch the NASA spacecrafts into orbit. But we do have the ability to perform every step of the process for other missions.

You've previously said that one of Rocket Lab's primary goals is to help "democratize space." What does this mean to you?

When I started the company in 2006, [space travel and technology] was pretty much the domain of the government. You know, there was SpaceX and a few other small commercial companies that started around the same time as we did. But it was very much dominated by large government institutions, and any commercial enterprise in space was very fringe. Throughout the length of my career, though, I've started to witness the growing, vast democratization of space. Most of the launch vehicles in the U.S. are commercially owned now. Rocket Lab has the second most frequently launched rocket in the U.S. And the most frequently launched rocket in the U.S., SpaceX's Falcon 9, is of course also from a commercial company.

How does space technology help inform experts about climate change?
Satellites and other space technology have been the backbone of climate modeling and understanding for decades. I can even remember watching TV when I was young and, you know, someone onscreen would go, "And now we cut to satellite imagery," and it would show all this cloud coverage and Earth and whatnot. This was back in the 1980s. So it's been a cornerstone of climate predictions, and PREFIRE is a good example of this. It's a mission to really understand rising sea levels and melting ice sheets in the Arctic and Antarctic. The satellites have infrared sensors that can track heat loss, which ultimately indicates how much ice has melted and is lost to the ocean. This information really refines models and helps provide more accurate sea-level-rise predictions.

The unique thing is that in order for these satellites to provide the level of accuracy, resolution and precise measurements that [climate scientists] need, we need to launch the two of them into somewhat different orbits. This is where Electron as a small, reusable rocket really comes into its own. Normally if you wanted to send spacecraft into two separate orbits, you'd also need two separate rockets. You'd have to typically procure a $60-million rocket, making the launches around $120 million total. And these satellites are, you know, about the size of a shoebox. It'd be very difficult to justify that kind of expenditure and resources for such small spacecraft.

Manufacturing space technology and launching rockets requires a lot of greenhouse gas emissions. Is it a good thing for the climate if more organizations can start accessing space?
I think that you have to just put it into context. To get these two satellites into orbit, we used about the same amount of jet fuel

as one Boeing 737 flight from Los Angeles to San Francisco. So for that exchange of carbon, which is pretty tiny in the grand scheme of things, we get pretty large science. The fact of the matter is that when you go to space, you have to burn stuff. But it's burned at such high pressures and temperatures that the combustion products are very efficient. Unfortunately, you can't do anything in space without some kind of emissions, and so you have to make those trades. Fortunately, with space travel, usually the missions that you're doing and the services that you're providing outweigh the cost significantly. I tend to think that putting stuff in space is like building infrastructure. If we put a satellite into orbit to do weather prediction, for example, that small machine provides weather details and data to literally millions of people around the planet. So you can have a really big impact for a relatively small piece of infrastructure. Whereas if you build a road in a city, it's only the people who live in that area and have access to it who benefit.

How does Rocket Lab try to limit its production of space junk?

It's a real challenge. Everything that goes into orbit generally leaves some kind of debris behind. And it's a bit of a misnomer that all the debris in orbit are considered spacecraft when, actually, there's a large portion of those debris that is, in fact, old, spent rocket pieces. So when we developed Electron we were determined to do our very best to avoid that kind of debris being left behind wherever possible. Fortunately space is very big, but it's going to get only busier in orbit, and the result of spacecrafts colliding is pretty significant. It's difficult to get governments together to agree on a set of rules about anything, but I do really think that there needs to be some form of cohesive space traffic management.

As the space travel and technology sector "democratizes," it also becomes more competitive. Do you think that this high level of competition is "good" for science?

Absolutely. Prior to Electron, you would've had to procure a Minotaur or Pegasus rocket–the only small, dedicated launch vehicles available at the time–for somewhere between $35 million and $50 million. The sticker price of an Electron launch is $7.5 million. That's competition for you. Those two other vehicles are now largely extinct since Electron's creation, but it's a great example of how competition has really enabled many more missions. Take our CAPSTONE [Cislunar Autonomous Positioning System Technology Operations and Navigation Experiment] project with NASA from two years ago as an example. That was a $10-million [launch] to the moon. That's crazy! So, yeah, competition is great.

How would you like to see Rocket Lab evolve over the next several years?

The ultimate goal for us is to become the end-to-end space company that makes space far more accessible and that makes these kinds of climate change missions even more feasible. At the moment the space industry is still very bifurcated. You have to be an expert in spacecraft and know all these things about space to be able to provide a service on Earth. But consolidating that into a single company that researchers, commercial customers and governments can just go to and ask for missions is the idea. I think that's what large, successful space companies of the future are going to look like. That's how we make these missions frequent, accessible and affordable.

About the Author

Riis Williams is a New York City–based science journalist who specializes in climate, health and wildlife reporting. She formerly served as Scientific American's news intern.

40 Years After Challenger Disaster, NASA Faces Safety Fears on Artemis II

By Meghan Bartels

Forty years ago today, disaster struck NASA's human spaceflight program when the space shuttle *Challenger* exploded 73 seconds after blastoff, killing all seven people onboard.

The tragedy nearly brought the shuttle program to an early end. Decades later, the mistakes that led to the *Challenger* disaster, as well as fallout from the similar 2003 loss of the shuttle *Columbia*, loom particularly large now, as NASA seeks to launch four astronauts on the ambitious *Artemis II* mission around the moon as early as next week.

The mission will be the first crewed flight of the massive Space Launch System (SLS) rocket and Orion capsule, as well as the first time that humans have left Earth's orbit since the final Apollo mission in 1972. Already NASA has faced public scrutiny over its handling of unexpected behavior from Orion's heat shield–crucial equipment to protect astronauts as they return to Earth–during an uncrewed orbital test flight in 2022.

NASA believes that changes made as a result of *Challenger* and other disasters in its history are enough to keep Artemis crews safe. "Challenger ... brought out aspects of the agency which hopefully no longer exist and which we are always working toward addressing," says Tracy Dillinger, safety culture program manager at NASA's Office of Safety and Mission Assurance. "Space is risky. We know that, and our astronauts know that. We just want to be smart about the risks that we accept." Currently, the Orion heat shield is widely believed to be the biggest risk to the crew; NASA has said the concern is addressed by changes to the *Artemis II* flight path.

From Routine to Disaster

The 1986 *Challenger* disaster occurred on the STS-51L mission, the 25th flight in NASA's shuttle program, which was approaching its fifth anniversary. During the weeklong mission, crew had an eclectic agenda–observe Halley's Comet and deploy both a communications satellite and an astronomical instrument into Earth orbit–but was most notable for one of its crew, Christa McAuliffe.

McAuliffe had taught middle and high school and was selected to fly after a nationwide "Teacher in Space" competition. She planned to teach two lessons from orbit, and her inclusion was part of a broader campaign by NASA to portray shuttle spaceflight as an ordinary, low-risk activity that nonastronauts could take part in.

"It's sort of an all-purpose carryall vehicle often referred to by the astronauts themselves as a space truck," says Jennifer Levasseur, a space historian and curator at the Smithsonian Institution's National Air and Space Museum. "The space shuttle is intended to be very regular, it's meant to be routine, it's meant to be safe–so safe that the astronauts don't even have to wear spacesuits."

On that chilly late January morning, thanks to the excitement around McAuliffe's flight, some 2.5 million students nationwide tuned in to watch the launch–only to see disaster unfold on live television. The so-called O-rings that joined the cylindrical segments of one of the shuttle's solid rocket boosters failed under launch conditions far colder than they'd been designed for. Just more than a minute after ignition, the ruptured booster caused the shuttle's giant external fuel tank to explode, tearing the vehicle to pieces over the ocean and dooming all seven astronauts.

Engineering Safety Culture

With the world watching, NASA scrambled to figure out what went wrong and how to fix it–all while wading into a deeper debate:

Was human spaceflight still worth the risk of catastrophic loss? Although NASA rejected calls to end the space shuttle program, it paused flights for nearly three years as it pored over data from the *Challenger* disaster.

With diagrams, charts and dense technical writing–in a report that spanned more than 200 pages, not including its 15 appendices–NASA officials deconstructed the failure. That document highlighted not only the thermal constraints of the O-rings but also the design limitations inherent to the shuttle and the sociological pressures surrounding the program that put those O-rings in place and drove the launch forward.

"It was very apparent on multiple missions prior to STS-51L that there was an issue with the solid rocket booster sections and the way they joined together," Levasseur says. Some safety concerns were even expressed before any shuttle ever flew. And on the morning of launch, when an engineer said he worried about the O-rings in the chilly weather, program managers who wanted the agency to successfully fly shuttles routinely decided to let the launch proceed anyway.

"Despite all of that knowledge, NASA was pressing ahead," Levasseur says. "Its management said, 'We have a schedule.'" That "launch fever" or "go fever," as well as recurring O-ring anomalies that lulled managers into overlooking them, emerged as the true downfall of *Challenger*. Extreme cold made the O-rings fail, but NASA's culture was just as blameworthy and needed a retrofit more urgently than any piece of shuttle hardware.

Smaller versions of NASA's *Challenger* investigation play out today, says Sandra Magnus, a part-time professor of the practice of engineering at the Georgia Institute of Technology and former NASA astronaut who previously served on NASA's Aerospace Safety Advisory Panel. "Whenever there's a mishap, whether it's something huge like *Challenger* or something a little bit less life-threatening, NASA has a process of going through, trying to understand what happened and why it happened," she says.

The Ambitions of Artemis

Now NASA is facing its first crewed journey beyond Earth's orbit since 1972, and many iterations of the agency's safety investigations processes have occurred along the path to launch to protect four astronauts: NASA's Reid Wiseman, Victor Glover and Christina Koch and the Canadian Space Agency's Jeremy Hansen. They will be the first humans to launch on the SLS megarocket and its Orion capsule, and if all goes smoothly, they will set a record for humans reaching the farthest distance from Earth.

Some worry how they will fare during their return home, when their capsule must re-enter and traverse Earth's thick atmosphere, enveloped for long, nail-biting minutes in a friction-kindled fireball. Orion is equipped with a heat shield, of course–one that combines updates based on knowledge from both Apollo and the space shuttle program, Levasseur notes.

Examining the Orion capsule that flew on the uncrewed *Artemis I* mission in 2022, NASA officials noticed that huge chunks of its heat shield had unexpectedly blown away. It's an issue engineers have been investigating in the years since the test flight, and they say that adjusting Orion's path toward Earth–plunging faster through the atmosphere at a steeper incline instead of a shallower, more prolonged descent–should safeguard against the problem.

But that's not the same as redesigning the heat shield, and the agency opted not to test the heat shield on this new reentry profile before committing *Artemis II*'s astronauts to it. Redesigning the heat shield, NASA officials say, would have caused too much delay, and a new reentry test was deemed too expensive.

An observer would be hard put to determine whether that choice reflects launch fever once again breaking through procedural norms. Artemis is a massive program–NASA estimated in 2024 that its costs since October 2011 would reach $93 billion by October 2025–and that can inherently bring pressure to keep things moving, says Jordan Bimm, a space historian at the University of Chicago.

And NASA has plenty of pressures to juggle. "NASA's never been in a moment like this before," Bimm says. Across the horizon of spaceflight, the agency is juggling negotiating multibillion-dollar contracts with commercial giants such as SpaceX and Blue Origin, while competing with relative newcomers to spaceflight, such as China and India, that are pursuing their own crewed ambitions.

The agency set what experts say was a promising example during the *Artemis I* mission, which was repeatedly delayed, including even rolling the massive rocket off the launchpad to shelter it from a hurricane.

For Levasseur, that suggests the people leading NASA today will make the hard choices that keep their crews safe. "They're people who were children or young people during the 1980s, who were inspired by the early space shuttle flights," she says. Many, like her, were shaped by watching the *Challenger* disaster as a child, or by the later *Columbia* tragedy. "Those memories are there, and they're not going to want to make the same mistakes that were made before."

About the Author

Meghan Bartels is a science journalist based in New York City. She joined Scientific American *in 2023 and is now a senior reporter there. Previously, she spent more than four years as a writer and editor at Space.com, as well as nearly a year as a science reporter at Newsweek, where she focused on space and Earth science. Her writing has also appeared in* Audubon, Nautilus, Astronomy *and* Smithsonian, *among other publications. She attended Georgetown University and earned a master's degree in journalism at New York University's Science, Health and Environmental Reporting Program.*

Astronauts Return to Earth in First ISS Medical Evacuation

By Claire Cameron

One of the most notable chapters in the history of NASA is coming to something like a close: after calling for an unprecedented medical evacuation of four astronauts onboard the International Space Station (ISS), these space farers are safely home. The episode has left myriad unanswered questions about what exactly happened to prompt the stunning decision to end their mission early–a first in the history of the ISS.

When asked at a Thursday press conference if NASA planned to release further information about the medical situation that prompted the evacuation, agency chief Jared Isaacman said it is "very committed to being transparent."

"There are some medical privacy considerations here. That said, to the extent that we are in a position to share more information publicly and have the necessary consent, we would do so," he said.

"Obviously, we took this action because it was a serious medical condition," Isaacman said. "The astronaut in question is fine right now, in good spirits and going through the proper medical checkouts."

Crew-11 splashed down in a SpaceX Crew Dragon capsule off the coast of California at approximately 3:41 A.M. EST. The evacuating Crew-11 includes NASA astronauts Mike Fincke and Zena Cardman, Japanese Aerospace Exploration Agency astronaut Kimiya Yui and Russian cosmonaut Oleg Platonov. NASA has not identified which of these astronauts experienced the medical issue. "The crew member of concern is doing fine. We will share updates on their health as soon as it's appropriate to do so," Isaacman said on Thursday.

The crew is undergoing medical evaluation on a receiver ship and is headed to a hospital in San Diego, Calif., for further investigation and care, said Joel Montalbano, deputy associate administrator of NASA's Space Operations Missions Directorate, at the same conference.

Whatever happened to Crew-11 could influence how the agency prepares for future human spaceflight missions, including the upcoming *Artemis II* moon flyby. NASA will conduct a full debrief and review of the Crew-11 mission, Isaacman said.

"When we go through the debrief on this, we're going to learn a lot about the things we got right and did it very well and make sure we apply that in other applications going forward," Isaacman said.

The ISS is equipped with an array of medical equipment, drugs and diagnostic tools—all of which the station's crew know how to use. That means most minor ailments can be dealt with onboard: wounds can be sutured, blood can be taken and ultrasounds can be done. But NASA evidently decided that whatever occurred was serious enough that the ISS was not the place to keep the ailing astronaut. The agency plans for these contingencies on every mission, Isaacman said.

"There are early return options on *Artemis II*. There are options to bring astronauts back from the space station in hours, not days. So I think that the fact that we did take some extra time here does speak to the stability of the situation," he said.

About the Author

Claire Cameron is breaking news chief at Scientific American. *Originally from Scotland, she moved to New York City in 2012. Her work has appeared in* National Geographic, Slate, Inc. Magazine, Nautilus, Semafor, *and elsewhere.*

Crew-11 Astronauts Reflect on ISS Medical Evacuation and Future of Human Spaceflight

By Claire Cameron

Just a week after their unprecedented return to Earth following a medical issue onboard the International Space Station, the four members of Crew-11 presented a united front, indicating that the future of human spaceflight was bright.

At a press conference on Wednesday, former ISS commander and NASA astronaut Mike Fincke said that the way the crew and ground teams came together to deliver the four astronauts safely back to Earth showed how well prepared humans are to continue to explore space.

"How we handled everything all the way through ... nominal operations to this unforeseen operation really bodes well for future exploration," Fincke said. "So when we're getting ready for Artemis, I am very optimistic."

Fincke is one of the four returned crew members–the others are NASA's Zena Cardman, Japan Aerospace Exploration Agency (JAXA) astronaut Kimiya Yui and Russian cosmonaut Oleg Platonov–who were rushed back to Earth weeks ahead of schedule. On Wednesday, the four offered scant details of what exactly happened to trigger their early return to Earth–the first in the history of the ISS.

Fincke said the issue arose as he and Cardman were preparing to undertake a space walk–which would have been Cardman's first–outside the ISS. Fincke also said that the ISS's portable ultrasound machine was used to respond to the medical issue.

"So when we had this emergency, the ultrasound machine came in super handy," Fincke said, adding the caveat that the ISS does not have the ability to house larger imagers, such as magnetic resonance imaging machines.

"We do try to make sure that everybody, before we fly, are really, really not prone to surprises. But sometimes things happen, and surprises happen," Fincke said.

JAXA's Yui praised his international colleagues for the response to the medical issue. "We can handle any kind of difficult situation," he said. "This is actually very, very good experience for the future of human spaceflight."

Looking beyond low-Earth orbit, Cardman said she did not think future crews on the ISS would necessarily need new or additional training in light of what happened to Crew-11. But, she said, missions beyond the ISS, to the moon or even further out in space, presented a different question. "I think the farther afield we go as we journey beyond low-Earth orbit, having tools on board to diagnose and treat a myriad of situations is going to be a really interesting problem to solve," she said.

Cardman emphasized the ISS's pioneering role in human spaceflight. Looking ahead to future space exploration and science expeditions, "we're going to need astronauts to be the eyes and ears and lab notebook for the researchers on the ground," she said.

"We're not always going to be the scientific experts. In fact, we rarely will be," Cardman said. "The ISS has been an excellent proving ground for how we get science done."

About the Author

Claire Cameron is breaking news chief at Scientific American. *Originally from Scotland, she moved to New York City in 2012. Her work has appeared in* National Geographic, Slate, Inc. Magazine, Nautilus, Semafor, *and elsewhere.*

NASA Evacuation of ISS Highlights How Astronauts Prepare for Medical Emergencies in Space

By Claire Cameron

NASA's unprecedented decision to prematurely end a mission to the International Space Station (ISS) because of a sick astronaut is shining a light on how the agency prepares for medical problems and emergencies in space.

The decision, announced by NASA's new administrator Jared Isaacman during a press briefing on Thursday, marks the first time any space agency has ordered a medical evacuation of an ISS mission.

"Statistically, it probably should have happened many times by now over the last 25 years that we've had people on the International Space Station," says former NASA astronaut Andrew Feustel, who was commander of an ISS mission while he was at the agency and is now lead astronaut at the private space company Vast. "But it hasn't, and part of that speaks to the level of medical screening that's done, at least currently, on government professional career astronauts before they fly in space."

It also speaks to the preparedness of astronauts and the space station to deal with medical issues that arise. In orbit at least 370 kilometers above Earth, the ISS houses various medical equipment, from an ultrasound to IVs to a defibrillator, that can be used to diagnose and treat crew members who get sick or injured. It also carries an extensive array of drugs, including anesthetics, antisickness medication, hydration liquids and antibiotics.

"You can do things like administer oxygen to somebody. You can do wound care. There's a whole pharmacy basically onboard," says Jordan Bimm, a space historian and an assistant professor at the University of Chicago.

There are, however, limits to how much equipment the station can hold. There is neither a magnetic resonance imaging (MRI) machine to scan crew members nor enough supplies or space to perform extensive surgeries. Even so, Catherine Coleman, a former astronaut and author of the book *Sharing Space*, says she practiced gallbladder removal as part of her training, despite not being a medical professional. (The ISS does not currently have the equipment to perform such a surgery in orbit.)

Crews are extensively briefed on how to use all the equipment on the ISS and when needed they work with teams of doctors on the ground to talk through any medical issues that come up–a system Coleman compares to telemedicine on Earth.

Astronauts in line to go to the ISS spend weeks with doctors across different disciplines, including emergency medicine and dentistry, Coleman says. She and her colleagues learned how to put in IVs, insert a catheter, do a tracheostomy to create an airway and perform lifesaving techniques such as cardiopulmonary resuscitation (CPR).

"We're doing things like that with great supervision, but we're actually doing them so that, if it comes up, we're ready to do them," she says. Once astronauts are onboard the ISS, surgeons on the ground regularly talk to them about their health and tell them how to perform medical procedures as needed. Importantly, she says, that kind of close communication was likely key to the care and decision to bring home the stricken Crew-11 member.

Yet despite such coaching, being in the microgravity environment of orbit complicates even the most routine of procedures, Coleman says. The station is equipped with a stretcher with straps to hold crew members in place, should they require it for a procedure. And on her first day at the station, Coleman recalls working out how she would perform CPR in near weightlessness.

"Some people, it's the knees under the stretcher, and then they're going to be compressing on top using their stomach muscles," she says. "It depends on the person, if that is going to be enough force or not."

Microgravity also muddies the body's baseline for health. Fluid moves differently in the body while in space, leading many crew members to feel stuffy, for example, or to experience headaches and backaches. The space station environment is also known to alter some astronauts' vision in orbit or once back on Earth, and may cause cardiovascular changes, too. Crew members collect regular blood and urine samples, and they often take part in medical experiments while in orbit, making them very much in tune with their health.

"We are lab rats up there, and so we're really taught to be actively thinking about how we're doing," Coleman says.

But the best laid plans can go awry. And perhaps nowhere is that truer than in an extreme environment such as space.

"We don't have an operating room on ISS, and we really don't have all of the support infrastructures that we need for any major complications," former ISS mission commander Feustel says. "The fallback method for a low-Earth-orbit station, which is, you know, [more than] 350 kilometers above the surface, is to just come home."

And that is what is happening for Crew-11. While the sick crew member's status was described by NASA chief Isaacman as "stable" on Thursday, the decision to bring them back to Earth would not have been made lightly.

"It clearly went to the top of the organization," Coleman says. "It's nontrivial to decide you're going to end a space mission, given how much effort is put into executing one in the first place."

About the Author

Claire Cameron is breaking news chief at Scientific American. *Originally from Scotland, she moved to New York City in 2012. Her work has appeared in* National Geographic, Slate, Inc. Magazine, Nautilus, Semafor, *and elsewhere.*

Igloos on Mars? How Future Astronauts Could Use Ice to Survive

By Claire Cameron

If humans are ever to land on Mars, they will need somewhere to stay—a protective shell that can shield them from the sun's harsh rays. One possible answer: great, glassy domes of ice.

Mars is rich in ice, both on and under its surface—with more predicted to lie farther below its dusty exterior. If future astronauts were able to access it, they could use that ice to build hardy shelters, according to new preliminary research presented on Tuesday at the annual meeting of the American Geophysical Union.

Each structure could range from a few tens of square meters to a couple of hectares in size with a domed roof and space for living and growing food for sustenance. Designed to be entirely clear, the domes would let in sunlight but not harmful ultraviolet rays from the sun, says Robin Wordsworth, an earth and planetary sciences professor at Harvard University and a co-author of the new research. "Sunlight is particularly important to grow plants without artificial lighting and for human psychology," he says.

The proposal could solve a major problem that any future crewed Mars mission would need to confront: how to build and supply a safe habitat for humans. Elon Musk's SpaceX is attempting to tackle the issue, at least in part, with its Starship rocket program. Starship is designed to haul 100 metric tons of cargo into space, which means it could feasibly bring building materials with it. But it is still in development. And even if SpaceX does make it to Mars, the company will likely need to send many rockets at a time to support a human mission there.

For the new research, the scientists used mathematical models to work out the amount of ice that would be needed for the habitats. Combined with exterior coatings, that could warm their interior to a livable temperature of around 68 degrees Fahrenheit (20 degrees Celsius), according to Wordsworth.

Certainly, communities from across our planet have harnessed ice in similar ways before. In addition to the igloos built by some Inuit in the Arctic, people have lived in ice caves and other shelters that offer warmth, stability and protection from the weather.

What is less clear, however, is how future Mars astronauts would be able to gather enough ice to build anything. Wordsworth points out that, although his team's idea requires a lot of ice, it's easier to process and extract than other materials, such as silica, that could be used to build structures on Mars.

It's also unclear how crews would protect their igloos from Mars's famous dust storms, which could interfere with the structures' insulating effect. Wordsworth admits that the storms present a serious challenge.

"We haven't addressed dust directly yet," he says, "but compressed air jets blown onto the surface of the dome following a dust storm would be one possible solution."

About the Author

Claire Cameron is breaking news chief at Scientific American. *Originally from Scotland, she moved to New York City in 2012. Her work has appeared in* National Geographic, Slate, Inc. Magazine, Nautilus, Semafor, *and elsewhere.*

It's Nearly Time to Say Goodbye to the International Space Station. What Happens Next?

By Jonathan O'Callaghan

Human spaceflight is on the cusp of an intriguing new dawn. For 25 years, astronauts have lived and worked onboard the International Space Station (ISS), starting with the arrival of its first occupants on November 2, 2000. Built through a partnership between the U.S. and Russia in the aftermath of the cold war, the ISS has now witnessed five presidential administrations, the advent and demise of the iPod and even the lofting of another orbital habitat, China's Tiangong space station. But the ISS's days are numbered. By 2031, NASA plans to deorbit the space station. Citing aging hardware and rising costs, the agency will bring it back through Earth's atmosphere for a fiery plunge into the Pacific Ocean.

If all goes as planned, commercial space stations–outposts operated not by government agencies but instead by private companies–will take the ISS's place to build on its success. The first of these is set to launch next year, with a slew of others scheduled to follow soon after. All of them have the same goal of fostering a vibrant, human-centered economy in Earth orbit–and ultimately beyond.

"We hope to build habitats for the moon [and] Mars and eventually even an artificial-gravity space station," says Max Haot, CEO of Vast, a Long Beach, Calif.-based company at the forefront of the private-sector spacefaring push. Vast plans to launch its Haven-1 space station as soon as May 2026. On Haven-1's heels will be several other habitats from Axiom Space, Blue Origin and Starlab Space. All of them are intended to reach orbit by the end of the decade (and are still somewhat reliant on NASA as a paying customer).

The ISS will leave behind an important legacy, says Bill Nelson, who was formerly a U.S. senator and a space shuttle crew member, as well as NASA's administrator from 2021 to 2025, and formalized the time line for the nation's pivot to commercial space stations. "The station has done incredible things," he says, from establishing how to live safely in space to exploring the promise and peril of microgravity environments. All the while, the ISS has been a shining beacon of global cooperation.

NASA's shift from "operator" of the ISS to a "tenant" on space stations, Nelson says, should help the agency focus on more innovative and daring explorations deeper in the solar system. "It's part of the evolution of space," he adds. "It used to be all government. Now we have commercial partners and international partners."

Some have argued that the ISS could still have a long life ahead if it were to be boosted to a higher orbit, where it could endure intact for decades or centuries. "I think it's the most amazing thing that humanity has ever constructed," says Greg Autry, a space policy expert at the University of Central Florida. "It's kind of like deorbiting Buckingham Palace. It's an amazing historical structure, and it should be recognized for that." NASA, however, determined that rescuing the ISS would be too costly and complex. Instead the space agency opted to pay SpaceX nearly $1 billion to develop a vehicle that will push the station back into Earth's atmosphere in 2031, leaving China's Tiangong space station as the only government-run outpost in orbit.

By the time that happens, multiple commercial space stations could be active. Haven-1, the first of them, is a singular, shipping-container-sized structure that will be launched on a SpaceX Falcon 9 rocket. Initially lofted uncrewed, the station will offer stays of up to 10 days for both governmental and private-sector visitors, all of whom are planned to reach Haven-1 via a SpaceX Dragon capsule. The cost of a private booking is undisclosed at present.

"Our core business model is 85 percent sovereign space agencies, including NASA, and then maybe 15 percent private individuals,"

Haot says. Onboard, four occupants will have private sleeping berths with inflatable beds, a domed window to observe Earth and high-speed Internet provided by SpaceX's Starlink service. A built-in science lab will allow them to conduct research at the station.

Haven-1 is a precursor to a much bigger construct planned by Vast called Haven-2, which is expected to launch by the time the ISS is abandoned. Haven-2 will comprise multiple Haven-1-style modules arranged in a cross shape to enable a continuous human presence in orbit rather than short stays like Haven-1 will host. It will be joined by the other commercial ventures–Axiom Station, Blue Origin's Orbital Reef, and Starlab.

New priorities may come with any new private era in Earth orbit. Whereas the ISS was notionally a station focused on science, private habitats will inevitably have a broader purview, from acting as proverbial space hotels to being manufacturing hubs for products imported back to Earth. "You can make much better silicon crystals [for semiconductors] in space," says Autry, listing one of several perennial arguments for more industrial activity in orbit. "[There are] a lot of different economic drivers that I think will eventually pay off," and the space tourism business "will be much larger than most people believe."

Autry points to Blue Origin's New Shepard rocket, which launches paying customers straight up and down on suborbital rides lasting just 10 minutes but has already flown about 80 people (including some repeat customers). "There's a really strong demand," he says, arguing that an increase in rides to space–and destinations to reach–shows space tourism can "absolutely" be as accessible as other extreme environments, such as the deep sea. "There's no reason you can't get suborbital ticket prices into the thousands of dollars and orbital ticket prices under $1 million," he says. "I think it will happen in the next 10 to 20 years."

What role science will play on commercial space stations will, to some degree, depend on the tools customers can use onboard. Already the major players have suggested an assortment of relevant, high-grade laboratory equipment will be the norm. Fabrizio Fiore, an astrophysicist at the Astronomical Observatory of Trieste in Italy, says this means more opportunities for scientists to conduct research that was logistically impossible on the ISS. "Even putting a small thing on [the ISS] is very, very time-consuming and difficult," he says. "If we are going to have space stations that are not dedicated to governmental astronauts, it will be much easier to build experiments on them."

Research institutions and universities could increase their access to space, too, perhaps by sending their own astronauts. Earlier this year, for example, Purdue University booked tickets for a 2027 flight on Virgin Galactic's suborbital space plane for a pair of its researchers. It's not unfathomable to think the same might occur on commercial space stations, especially if the cost of visiting them can be brought down to a reasonable level.

In the bigger picture, some see the rise of private space stations as part of a turning point for life itself. Caleb Scharf, an astrobiologist in the U.S., argues in his new book *The Giant Leap* that space exploration is a next step in the evolution of humankind. "The capacity to put objects into orbit around Earth, and study Earth from space, is this unique perspective that no other organism has ever had in the history of life on Earth in the last four billion years," he says. "Getting into space is another major evolutionary transition point. You can imagine, if we do spread out across the solar system in the centuries to come, that will induce fundamental changes on us as a species. It will dilute us. It will disperse us. We will undergo speciation. While we now call ourselves 'humans' as a single species, the future may be many species that were derived from what we are today."

Commercial space stations, Scharf says, might be the next step in this journey–but he's not quite ready to buy a ticket–or the hype. "Maybe we'll learn that commercial space stations are the best thing ever," he says. "Or perhaps we will discover that this isn't actually the be all and end all. It's absolutely possible that commercial space stations, for economic or financial reasons, do not yield what is expected or hoped."

By the end of the decade, humans are also planned to return to the moon in competing efforts, one led by the U.S. and the other led by China. Ian Crawford, a planetary scientist at Birkbeck, University of London, has previously argued that space stations can be a distraction from this endeavor. "To talk about space exploration properly, we have to move away from low-Earth orbit," he says. "How 'space hotels' in Earth orbit really feed into that, I don't know."

Whatever direction these new stations take, they will mark the end of a historic experiment–a full quarter-century (and counting) of humans living and working off-world. The feat is all the more remarkable for how unremarkable it now appears: More than 40 percent of all the people on Earth are younger than the ISS, having never known a world without it. For many of them, the station's quiet technical triumph of unbroken orbital occupation is understandably banal, boring and routine. That is to say, like so many wondrous things we take for granted, it seems the ISS won't really be understood for its good until it's gone.

About the Author

Jonathan O'Callaghan is an award-winning freelance journalist covering astronomy, astrophysics, commercial spaceflight and space exploration. Follow him on X @ Astro_Jonny

Private Space Stations of the Future Promise Luxury. But Can They Deliver?

By Sarah Scoles

NASA wants to get out of the space station business and put it in the hands of, well, businesses. The agency is planning to send the International Space Station (ISS) to a fiery death through Earth's atmosphere in 2031 so it can focus on its longer-term, farther-out (literally) goals such as going back to the moon. Elon Musk recently called for the agency to deorbit the station much sooner.

But agency officials are hoping humans will still have a future in Earth orbit through NASA's Commercial Low Earth Orbit Development program. The initiative has commissioned private companies to come up with their own flashy corporate solutions to in-space stays.

Those stations could house astronauts from the U.S. as well as other countries. Furthermore, both NASA and the space station makers themselves are banking on the demand of other customers—private researchers, tourists and companies such as pharmaceutical firms—to stimulate a space economy that's sustainable with or without NASA money.

The program follows a model similar to the one that NASA has employed to develop astronaut-ferrying spacecraft after the space shuttles retired: the agency has been contracting with private companies such as SpaceX to shuttle cargo and astronauts to the ISS rather than owning and operating its own space vehicles.

So far, NASA has partnered with companies on three projects to design space stations as part of the program's first phase. A second phase is on the way, and at least one competitor is nipping at these companies' tail fins.

Axiom Station

A company called Axiom Space has been awarded more than $100 million from NASA to develop its station. And NASA isn't Axiom's only partner: the company has paired up with a motley crew, from beleaguered aerospace mainstay Boeing to satellite industry giant Maxar to Build-A-Bear–the stuffed animal company. Since 2022 Axiom has been sending missions of private astronauts on SpaceX capsules to the ISS. Over its three trips so far, its travelers have completed 105 research activities in life sciences, materials science and advanced manufacturing. A fourth mission is in the works.

The company has also sent Build-A-Bears in Axiom spacesuits along with the private astronauts. Unsurprisingly, you can buy a replica of those gravity-defying bears at Axiom's website.

Welding and machining of the space station's first module is in progress, and Axiom plans to launch its Payload Power Thermal Module (the station's version of a utility closet) to the ISS in 2027. After it's been berthed there for a while, the module will detach and go solo into space, where it will eventually be joined by two habitable modules: an airlock and a research and manufacturing facility. Voilà: a space station, likely with human and inanimate ursine residents.

But the interior decor is the big buzz around this station. Axiom didn't leave its aesthetics to engineers: it contracted with French architect and designer Philippe Starck, who has designed everything from a Russian oligarch's superyacht to Fossil watches to the insides of New York City's Paramount Hotel. With his creative touch, Axiom Station will have tufted, organic-looking walls embedded with color-switching LEDs.

Starck has said he envisions the environment like an egg, with materials and a color scheme meant to evoke the universe's fetushood–which, of course, invokes the movie *2001: A Space Odyssey* but hopefully not the travails of its protagonist. The shifting LEDs are also meant to blur the view of the outside universe with the station's interior. Or, as Starck's website puts it, "just as all the shades of lights and colors of day and night, the egg will also live to the mood and biorhythm of its osmotic inhabitant."

Fetal boarders will also have Wi-Fi, video and what Axiom has called "the largest window observatory ever constructed for the space environment." Axiom's press materials suggest the company is going after the luxury market; another of its projects, for instance, was a spacesuit collaboration with Prada.

Orbital Reef

Orbital Reef, the name of a planned home meant to bob safely in the ocean of space, is another of NASA's phase one selections. The project, which as of 2024 had won $172 million from NASA, is perhaps the most explosive of the future space stations. Last year and in late 2023 NASA blew up prototypes of the Reef's habitable module–called LIFE, for Large Integrated Flexible Environment–in what it called a "burst test."

LIFE won't have a stiff shell like other stations: it will inflate in orbit to three stories tall and 27 feet in diameter, and it will accommodate sleeping spaces for four astronauts, their science experiments and their exercise equipment, among other amenities. But NASA needed to find out how much pressure the habitat could handle before blowing, so it pumped it up until it burst apart in a spectacular show that resulted in a net of detritus that resembled a sea creature. LIFE reached 74 pounds per square inch in its test last year before it broke down–that's more than twice the pressure in a car tire.

The Reef is a partnership between Sierra Space and Blue Origin, Jeff Bezos's cosmic company. Given the multipurpose nature of Amazon, Bezos's most famous creation, maybe it's no surprise that Blue Origin describes the Reef as "a mixed-use business park 250 miles above Earth."

Amenities will include a medical center, robotics to help with future experiments, separate quarters for work and play and Sierra Space's trademarked Astro Garden system, which looks like a hipster coffee shop's vertical wall garden and could provide astronauts roughage (and the taste of home) on their journey.

Orbital Reef, if all goes as planned, could start operating by the end of the decade, focusing on science, research and tourism, in addition to accommodating governmental guests. With interior details handled by architecture firm Hassell–which has designed airport terminals, train stations, office buildings and zoos (mixed-use indeed!)–the station's central feature is a social hub where astronauts can gather. At its core is a table made for sitting in microgravity. The table appears to have a circular base on which astronauts can hook their feet to stay grounded.

Starlab

Starlab Space is a joint venture between aerospace giant Airbus and a company called Voyager Space. Importantly, Voyager is majority shareholder in the organization Nanoracks, which helps scientists' payloads make it to space and whose airlock, attached to the ISS, has deployed small satellites out of that station and into orbit. Now, as Starlab Space, these heavies, along with partners such as Mitsubishi– and MDA Space, which built the ISS's robotic arm–plan to build their own space station, called Starlab. The team, which announced a European subsidiary in January, is gunning for a 2028 launch and already boasts a NASA allocation of more than $200 million. In February, the Texas Space Commission also awarded the company $15 million. And it has a former NASA astronaut, Tim Kopra, at the helm.

"The ISS was probably the most incredible vehicle ever built," Kopra says. But rather than simply replacing that iconic station, he hopes to take lessons from that project and apply them to Starlab. One of those, he says, is the importance of international partnership–hence the multicompany cooperation. Beyond the core collaborators, the team also includes partners such as Palantir, which is creating a digital twin of the Starlab station—a software duplicate of the real deal, which allows engineers to model, monitor and predict onboard goings-on—and will use artificial intelligence to enhance operations (and hopefully not go rogue like HAL 9000).

Starlab will launch as a complete setup rather than doing so piecemeal, as was the case for the ISS. The ISS strategy, while necessary, was long and complicated, Kopra says. And it resulted in a kind of split architecture. "The way [the ISS was] built [was] with a bunch of very small cans," Kopra says—akin to having a house with many small rooms. That meant that the things astronauts needed could be scattered across the space, requiring them to surf microgravity from room to room to perform a task. That's not so for Starlab: "By having a large station like this, you can organize the equipment and inventory management in such a way that you minimize this extra time," he says.

Today Starlab Space has a partial mockup of the station and plans to install a full-size one this coming summer at NASA's Johnson Space Center in Houston. "We consider [NASA], and NASA considers themselves, as an anchor customer," Kopra says, "and we want to be close to where the expertise is."

For now, the company is focused on pursuing customers from among the official ranks of astronauts from places like the U.S., Europe, Japan and Canada. Company leaders believe only a few tourists might be interested. "We don't think that's a very large market, but we certainly have the capacity to support it," Kopra says. More likely customers are nongovernmental spacefarers who are scientists, whether from academia or industry—such as an investigator from a drug company that wants to develop new pharmaceuticals or someone who wants to experiment with semiconductors and maybe eventually do the manufacturing many miles above sea level.

To help make sure everyone, regardless of their cosmic goals, gets a good night's rest, Voyager Space has partnered with hotel bigwig Hilton, which, as the thinking goes, knows about extended stays. "Hilton is sharing insights into designing comfortable and functional sleep environments; creating communal spaces to foster connection and socialization, elevating wellness-focused design to go beyond what has been delivered on the International Space Station; and supporting aesthetic design, wayfinding and human ergonomics for crew quarters and shared areas," according to Larry Traxler, senior vice president of global design, Hilton. He did not specify whether continental breakfast was provided.

Haven

Aerospace firm Vast isn't currently part of the LEO Destinations program, but it does have existing agreements with the agency and is vying for a spot in the second phase of the private space station program. And the company may actually be the first to launch a station to space: it plans to send a prototype called Haven-1 to orbit in 2026.The company, along with SpaceX, recently reached out to scientific researchers seeking proposals for experiments about long-term human spaceflight.

Vast's initial habitat will have a volume of 45 cubic meters, about the size of an average kitchen in the U.S., and will resemble an Ikea studio put together without colorful options. This stylistic choice makes sense, given the designer Vast had in its Rolodex: Peter Russell-Clarke, whose creative touch informed the designs of iPhones, iPads, Macs and Apple Watches.

Haven's central feature will be a communal table that pops up and down, deploying on demand, like furniture in a space-saving recreational vehicle. A domed window that will be located right above, like a dining room skylight, will give astronauts that coveted view of space. Behind the table, where you might normally find a bookcase or framed photographs, Haven-1 will have a little laboratory. There, experimental payloads live in the wall, where they will look like cubed organizational bins. Additionally, astronauts will be able to stay connected using Starlink Internet.

But it's Haven-1's successor, Haven-2, that the company imagines will "succeed the International Space Station," as Vast's website puts it. The company, which is aiming to launch Haven-2 in 2028, designed it with 55 cubic meters of space—more like a master bedroom. But this module will be joined by others that will link together like Lincoln Logs. Vast plans to launch a new Haven every six months and to end up with a cross-shaped set of nine by 2032. At that point, experimental payloads will be located inside and outside, space vehicles will be able to visit, and astronauts will perform extravehicular activities. Those astronauts might include private types or official envoys from different countries. The Czech Republic and Vast have already signed a memorandum of understanding, a fuzzy document that nonetheless paves the path for putting Czech astronaut Aleš Svoboda closer to that communal table.

Future astronauts of all sorts don't yet know how—or if—any of these commercial habitats will shake out, what life will be like inside them, what mix of interests their inhabitants will have or if that mix will in fact prove sustainable. Given that the vehicles would be the first privately created and operated space stations, everything about them—besides which spiffy designers have had hands in their interiors—is unknown. First, designs, prototypes and flashy press release illustrations must be transformed into actual objects. Then those objects have to actually get to space. How much that will cost, how long that will take and whether there will be enough paying customers for any, let alone all, of them remain open questions—as does whether their bubble may someday burst like an overstressed LIFE habitat.

About the Author

Sarah Scoles is a Colorado-based science journalist and a contributing editor at Scientific American. Her newest book is Countdown: The Blinding Future of Nuclear Weapons *(Bold Type Books, 2024).*

NASA's Perseverance Rover Faces New Uncertainty on Mars

By Kendra Pierre-Louis, Lee Billings, Fonda Mwangi & Alex Sugiura

Kendra Pierre-Louis: For *Scientific American's Science Quickly*, I'm Kendra Pierre-Louis, in for Rachel Feltman.

In July of 2020, NASA engineers sent a rover named Perseverance hurtling into space.

And in pictures it kind of looked like the diminutive robot in the Disney-Pixar film *WALL-E*—just much, much larger.

Perseverance, however, has spent its nearly five years on Mars focused on a very different mission. Instead of collecting trash Perseverance has roamed the Red Planet collecting rock samples, with the goal, in part, of finding potential evidence of life on Mars. The plan is to send the samples back to Earth, where they'd undergo further study. But that project, known as Mars Sample Return, is hanging on by a thread.

To walk us through what's happening we are joined today by Lee Billings, a senior desk editor here at SciAm. Thanks for joining us, Lee.

Lee Billings: Kendra, it's great to be here, as always.

Pierre-Louis: You know, I think to begin can you tell us broadly about the mission that Perseverance was tasked with completing on Mars?

Billings: Sure, Perseverance landed on Mars in early 2021; it was launched in 2020. And it was a follow-up to Curiosity, another NASA Mars rover. But the point is, is that Perseverance's goal, it's kind of the apex of planning for something called Mars Sample Return, which has been going on for decades ...

Pierre-Louis: Mm-hmm.

Billings: You know, back to the 1990s, even back to the 1960s, if you look back on it.

And the whole core idea is: we can study rocks better here on Earth than we can on Mars because it's hard to lift or build a huge wet lab on another planet ...

Pierre-Louis: Mm-hmm.

Billings: It's easier to bring smaller little bits of stuff back here.

And so Perseverance was crucial to that–in, again, kind of a very incremental way–building on a lot of the missions that had come before, in that Perseverance is actually kind of where the rubber meets the road, so to speak, where NASA scientists and other scientists from other institutions had narrowed down a short list of places to go on Mars to look for potential signs of life. And then from that short list they actually found a place, called Jezero Crater, this 30-mile-wide–almost 30-mile-wide depression in Mars that used to harbor an ancient lake and river delta and all this stuff.

And that's where Perseverance landed–had a rather nail-biting landing with the Sky Crane from JPL [NASA's Jet Propulsion Laboratory] that involved rockets and wires [delivering] this thing down to the surface. And it's been there, again, for the past several years, gathering samples, using a lot of its onboard instrumentation to figure out which of the rocks, which of the parts of the environment around there are most interesting to bring back to Earth. And it has 43, I believe, sample tubes–that's how many it carries–and the idea is that, in each one of these sample tubes, it can deposit a little sample, a little bit of Mars, to bring back to Earth someday.

But you can see, Perseverance is really good at finding these samples and collecting these samples–it has no capability whatsoever to actually bring these things back to Earth. That's a whole separate, subsequent phase of the mission and the thing that's really become this very troublesome roadblock and obstacle now for the program at large.

Pierre-Louis: What's driving this fascination with Mars?

Billings: So the big question, of course, is: "Are we alone?" And Mars is right next door, relatively speaking, and it has a lot of indications that suggest that it really wasn't so bad for life as we know it billions of years ago. If you think about the Mars of four or three billion years ago, this was a time when we see abundant signs on the planet of flowing water, of thicker atmosphere.

Right now, let's be clear, Mars is a frozen, terrible place to live. It's a freeze-dried mud ball.

Pierre-Louis: It feels like you're describing my apartment. [Laughs.]

Billings: [Laughs.] Or parts of my house, for that matter. It's not a good place to live, despite what some people might say. But long ago you could imagine it actually not being so bad of a place to live, to the degree that we really don't necessarily know of someplace that has a relatively Earth-like—or Earth-adjacent, we might call [it]—environment in which we could imagine life as we know it being able to exist.

And of course, "life as we know it" doesn't just include podcasters talking to each other into microphones but also little, tiny, microscopic single-celled organisms, microbes, which is really what most people would think would be on Mars rather than, you know, little green men or some kind of strange polar bear that's gonna eat you.

Pierre-Louis: Or TikTok influencers.

Billings: That's right, even though sometimes they do seem like they're from Mars.

And so the, the core idea really driving all this is trying to figure out whether or not we're alone. Because if you think about it, if we can find—if we can show that there were microbes on Mars, that there were Martians, that the planet was once alive, that's huge because that would suggest that life gets started pretty easily and that it must be out there everywhere. If we can look at the planet right next door to us and we can see that it was a true so-called independent origin or second genesis that would be huge.

There is this one sample, or this one singular rock, that Perseverance has found on Mars: a big hunk of mudstone on the rim of this crater that used to harbor, billions of years ago, a big lake and, and riverine delta. [The rock is] called "Cheyava Falls," and it's filled with organic matter. That is stuff that's rich in carbon, the molecular backbone of life as we know it. That's a pretty important thing because where you see organics on Earth, you tend to see life.

It also displays very tantalizing patterns on its surface and in the matrix of the rock itself; they're called "poppy seeds" and "leopard spots." And in short we see rocks that have those same types of features on Earth, and they can be produced abiotically, through lifeless processes over lots of time via a little bit of heating and some chemistry, but most of the time, when we see them on Earth, they're due to little microbes, little bugs in the rock, that use iron minerals to get energy to drive their metabolism.

And so based on everything that Perseverance has seen of this rock and has studied from this rock it looks like the rock formed in conditions that are closer to what we'd expect for life to be there. So it's not something that happened via volcanic eruption or some sudden event like that it; it's rather like, okay, this mudstone was deposited on the bottom of this ancient lake billions of years ago and sat there, and at some point, somehow, these really curious marks and speckles got all over it. And the best explanation that we have right now for those marks and speckles is microbes munching on iron and other minerals inside the rock.

So the evidence for life beyond Earth may already literally be in hand–almost. Perseverance has taken samples of this rock. It has stored the sample. It is ready to come to Earth. All we need to do is go there and get it. And that could be the most epochal discovery in history, to know that we're actually not alone.

So that is the big thing, but it's not the only thing—a lot of people get hung up on this. Even if Mars Sample Return reveals no life at this site or no life anywhere on the planet after we've exhaustively looked everywhere somehow, we would still learn so much about Mars, and that's important because Mars is kind of giving us an idea of the limits of habitability that we will potentially someday encounter on our own planet. It's showing us how a planet dies. It shows us how a once-relatively-nice place decays into a not-so-nice place. And studying the mechanics of that and knowing how that happened is valuable for being good stewards of our own planet.

Pierre-Louis: And so one of the things that is putting Mars Sample Return kind of in limbo is this question of funding, correct?

Billings: That's correct, yes. Big time. Big time. Because of course, we've never launched anything from Mars before, and that's how you have to get the samples back to Earth. But that's expensive. How do you do it? How many stages are there? The plan of record, up until the past couple years, it was supposed to cost—phew, man, I think it was about $6 billion was how [much] it was supposed to cost ...

Pierre-Louis: I spend that on shoes. [Laughs.]

Billings: [Laughs.] I mean, you know, a billion here, a billion there pretty much adds up to real money. But obviously, that is a lot of money. What happened was that this plan, it involved first retrieving the samples with a second rover that goes there to retrieve the samples and then that rover bringing the samples from Perseverance, or from a cache where they've been dropped on the ground, back to a launch site or maybe just launching from that same platform; launching it up into orbit, where it would rendezvous with an orbiting spacecraft that would take in the sample, store it, secure it, and then blast it back to Earth, on a long journey back to Earth, where it would then, you know, land somewhere in the U.S. high desert, probably, of the Southwest U.S., and be collected and taken to specialized facilities that are all biohazarded up, right? You think of, like, *The Hot Zone* or other things, you know, the place that they go to study Ebola, stuff like that, that's the same kind of facility they would take this stuff to, just 'cause we don't really know for sure. And then they would–you know, scientists would painstakingly analyze it for years and years, and eventually, parts of the samples would probably be distributed to other institutions around the world, and we'd all learn a lot more about Mars.

But yes, the problem is getting it off the ground 'cause that takes a lot of money. An analysis that was done that basically showed it was behind schedule and over cost, and the costs were looking to be upwards of $11 billion, so, you know, nearly a double in the estimated price tag. And we were looking at samples not really getting back here until 2040 at the earliest. And the former administrator of NASA, former senator and shuttle astronaut Bill Nelson, outgoing from the Biden administration, said, "You know, that's just too long to wait. That's too much money. We gotta find a faster, better, cheaper way to do it." But he left the core decision-making on that to the Trump administration.

Pierre-Louis: So we're in 2025 now. It took Perseverance about six months to get to Mars. Why would it take 15 years for the samples to get back?

Billings: Well, one thing to think about is that planets revolve around the sun–"Oh, well, of course they do." But what that means is that they don't necessarily all revolve at the same rate, in lockstep with each other. About every two years you have an alignment between Earth and Mars that allows us to get there more easily, with less fuel from a rocket. You know, everything you take off the Earth into orbit costs money to get up there, and it's a pretty exorbitant price, even though the price is falling. And so the less fuel you need to burn to get to Mars the cheaper your mission's gonna be. So every two years is one thing to think about.

The other thing to think about is that we're still talking about huge pieces of hardware that are either being built or not fully built. So that includes things like, you know, the rover that's going to retrieve the samples from Mars, from wherever Perseverance has stored them or wherever Perseverance is. It includes whatever system you're going to use to launch that thing back into orbit. It may include, you know, the Earth-return vehicle—all these components. It even includes the facilities on the Earth, you know, biohazard-style facilities that I mentioned earlier, that are needed to make people feel safe to have this stuff on our planet. All that stuff is included, and so that takes time to do.

And it's the kind of thing where if you threw money at it in some kind of Apollo program "let's beat the Russians to the moon"-style race, you could do it much faster, yes. But the trouble is, is that that's not what NASA is anymore. NASA hasn't been that for a long time, so singularly focused. And it's not just a problem of, oh, a lack of political will or something. It's also the broader problem that because NASA's different, because it has so much more stuff in its portfolio, there was and is a real risk that throwing too much money at Mars Sample Return would come at the very direct cost of much less money for pretty much everything else, for instance, in planetary science. And there's so many cool things out there in the solar system to see, whether you're thinking about the moon of Jupiter Europa or various moons around Saturn, for instance, or even Venus, that it's a pretty hard ask, I think, to say, "Well, let's just put all our eggs in the Mars basket."

Pierre-Louis: So my understanding is the Biden administration, when they were like, "We're gonna look for alternative methods," they were really looking towards commercial space. And can we talk a little bit about kind of the push for Mars from the commercial side?

Billings: Absolutely. The rise of commercial space, the new era that we are in and advancing into, was a key factor, I think, in the political decision-making that happened that brought us to this crossroads moment for Mars Sample Return because it's undeniable that the rates of launches are soaring and there are more players, more capabilities than ever before, more competition than ever before, more ways to potentially get this done. And not all of them necessarily have to rely on tried-and-true legacy ways that have certain price tags and costs associated with them.

So for instance, people love to talk about SpaceX, and most of the focus is on how SpaceX might help NASA astronauts return to the moon as part of the Artemis program, and the cornerstone of that is this huge, immensely gigantic megarocket that's intended to be fully reusable, which is the first time in history we've ever tried to do that, really, called Starship, that they keep testing and that it keeps blowing up or falling apart, right? So one idea, for instance, was: maybe we can just, if Starship works out really well getting people to the moon, we can just co-opt one of those Starships and send it to Mars and plop it down, and it can do all sorts of things.

But SpaceX isn't the only game in town, right? So Blue Origin, the company from Jeff Bezos of Amazon fame, is also a launch provider. They have proposed something to NASA, some kind of Plan B that they could provide to try to get these samples home. Another example would be a dark horse, in that most people don't really know about it as much, is the company called Rocket Lab. The plan from Rocket Lab that they've publicized claims to be able to deliver the samples from Perseverance for a price of about $4 billion, rather than something like $6 billion or $11 billion or more. And we don't have those numbers for all the proposals, and there's more proposals than I'm mentioning from other commercial outfits. But the point is is that there is a very strong, compelling case to be made, I think, that we can indeed do much of this, if not all of this, for much cheaper than what was previously the plan of record.

Pierre-Louis: This has been lovely. Thank you so much for your time.
Billings: It's my pleasure, Kendra. Thanks for talking with me.

Pierre-Louis: That's all for today. Don't forget to tune in on Friday, when our associate books editor, Bri Kane, digs into whether we should be thinking about AI in terms of empires and colonialism with Karen Hao.

Science Quickly is produced by me, Kendra Pierre-Louis, along with Fonda Mwangi and Jeff DelViscio. This episode was edited by Alex Sugiura. Shayna Posses and Aaron Shattuck fact-check our show. Our theme music was composed by Dominic Smith. Subscribe to *Scientific American* for more up-to-date and in-depth science news.

For *Scientific American*, this is Kendra Pierre-Louis. See you next time!

About the Authors

Kendra Pierre-Louis is a climate reporter focusing on the science and social impacts of climate change. She has worked for Gimlet, Bloomberg News and Popular Science. Pierre-Louis is based in New York City.

Lee Billings is a science journalist specializing in astronomy, physics, planetary science, and spaceflight and is senior desk editor for physical science at Scientific American. He is author of a critically acclaimed book, Five Billion Years of Solitude: The Search for Life Among the Stars, which in 2014 won a Science Communication Award from the American Institute of Physics. In addition to his work for Scientific American, Billings's writing has appeared in the New York Times, the Wall Street Journal, the Boston Globe, Wired, New Scientist, Popular Science and many other publications. Billings joined Scientific American in 2014 and previously worked as a staff editor at SEED magazine. He holds a B.A. in journalism from the University of Minnesota.

Fonda Mwangi is an award-winning multimedia editor at Scientific American and producer of Science Quickly. She previously worked at Axios, the Recount and

WTOP News. She holds a master's degree in journalism and public affairs from American University in Washington, D.C.

Alex Sugiura is a Peabody and Pulitzer Prize–winning composer, editor and podcast producer based in Brooklyn, N.Y. He has worked on projects for Bloomberg, Axios, Crooked Media and Spotify, among others.

Athena, Next U.S. Commercial Moon Lander, Is Set for Spectacular Lunar Science

By Gayoung Lee

As the U.S. and China ramp up their 21st-century race to land humans on the moon, it's easy to overlook another aspect of lunar exploration that in many respects has become a "no contest": commercially built and operated missions.

As part of NASA's Commercial Lunar Payload Services (CLPS) program, private U.S. companies have been hurling a steady stream of innovative robotic landers at the moon in unmatched numbers. And that trend is set to continue later this month with the launch of the next CLPS mission, IM-2, from the private company Intuitive Machines. Launching from NASA's Kennedy Space Center on a SpaceX Falcon 9 rocket no earlier than February 26, IM-2 is the company's shot at redemption after its inaugural predecessor, IM-1, tilted askew during its touchdown early last year. This time IM-2's lander, Athena, will seek to stick its landing and ferry a robust array of science and technology experiments to the vicinity of Mons Mouton, a plateau near the lunar south pole.

Officials from NASA and Intuitive Machines confirmed the launch details and previewed the mission's science during a press briefing on February 7.

"The IM-2 mission is particularly special..., as it is largely dedicated to lunar technology demonstrations that are truly foundational to creating a U.S.-led lunar infrastructure," Niki Werkheiser, director for technology maturation at NASA's Space Technology Mission Directorate, said during the briefing. These demonstrations include NASA's PRIME-1 (Polar Resources Ice Mining Experiment 1), which is "capable of identifying and quantifying water [ice]" and other volatile substances in lunar soil thanks to a drill that can reach up a meter into the surface.

"Demonstrating that we can collect these volatiles using the tech demonstrations onboard will not only help us better understand the origins of our solar system, but they will also be useful to our future astronauts for in situ resources, including drinking water, breathing air and creating rocket fuel," added Nicky Fox, associate administrator of NASA's Science Mission Directorate, during the briefing.

Other key technologies onboard Athena are the Micro Nova Hopper and the Lunar Surface Communication System (LSCS), developed by Intuitive Machines and Nokia Bell Labs, respectively, as part of NASA's Tipping Point technology initiative. Nicknamed "Grace" after software pioneer Grace Hopper, the Micro Nova Hopper is intended to leap away from Athena sometime after the lander's touchdown and to embark on a series of incremental hops toward Crater H—a 20-meter-deep, permanently shadowed crater about half a kilometer away.* There it will poke around for any signs of volatiles at or under the surface.

"The purpose of the [hopper] demo is to show that we can reach extreme environments with technologies other than rovers," explained Trent Martin, senior vice president of space systems at Intuitive Machines, at the briefing. Nokia's LSCS, which uses the same 4G LTE communications technology as a smartphone, will keep all of Athena's payloads "online" and connected as they branch out on their respective objectives. "We are set up to handle the very large number of payloads that we have on this mission ... and supporting operations from around the world from different control centers for various payloads that are on the mission," Martin added.

But Athena is also helping to continue previous and ongoing missions. For instance, it carries a tiny, NASA-provided aluminum device called the Laser Retroreflective Array, or LRA, which the space agency intends to use as a node in a larger lunar network for more accurately pinpointing the locations of key moon landers. And on its rocket to the moon, Athena shares a ride with various secondary payloads, chief among them NASA's Lunar Trailblazer, a moon-orbiting satellite slated to provide sophisticated high-resolution maps of where water may lurk at or beneath the moon's airless surface.

Besides highlighting some of the mission's science at the briefing, officials also offered reassurances that Athena wouldn't succumb to the same faults that led its predecessor, the IM-1 lander, nicknamed Odysseus, to land lopsided on the moon. During its landing on February 22 of last year, Odysseus touched down about 30 degrees off-kilter, breaking a leg and falling on its side–in spite of the prelaunch glitches Intuitive Machines purported to have fixed.

"After the mission, we went through what we call the 'hot wash,'" Martin said at the briefing. "We identified 85 things that we need to go off and look at–10 of them were required to be implemented prior to our IM-2 mission–[and] we've actually implemented all 85 of those."

The team also made it so that an error margin up to 10 degrees from the intended trajectory will still allow for Athena to begin normal operations. If the trajectory is further off, Athena's functionality will depend on how it lands, Martin said. "If we are off–let's say something happened like last time, and we ended up on our side–obviously we would not be able to deploy drills," he admitted. "However, there are lots of instruments on all of those systems that we would still be able to operate, just like last time, [when] we were able to get quite a bit of the data from the instruments that were on the Odysseus lander, and we were able to send that back to Earth."

With Athena, "we're taking kind of novel technologies and turning them into institutionalized capabilities–and that's really important," Werkheiser said at the briefing. Given the heavily technology-centered nature of the IM-2 mission, technological blips are more or less an inevitable part of the whole scheme, she said. "If we learn what we need to learn [from failures], and we could only do that by doing what we're doing now, then that is a success for us."

About the Author

Gayoung Lee is a science journalist and former news intern and Games ace at Scientific American. A philosopher turned journalist, originally from South Korea, Lee is interested finding unexpected connections between life and different science, particularly in theoretical physics and mathematics. You can read more about her here: https://gayoung-lee.carrd.co

John McFall Is Breaking Barriers as the World's First Parastronaut

By Max Springer

John McFall, a Paralympic sprinter who later became an orthopedic and trauma surgeon, has had an esteemed career fueled by his intense drive and curiosity. Now he's adding yet another acclaimed career to the mix: astronaut.

Following a serious motorcycle accident when he was 19, doctors amputated McFall's right leg above the knee. With the use of a prosthetic leg, which he has worn ever since, he won a bronze medal in the 100-meter sprint event at the 2008 Paralympic Games, where he represented the U.K. In 2022, after a competitive selection process, the European Space Agency (ESA) inducted McFall into its astronaut corps, making him its first physically disabled member, or parastronaut. McFall was specifically chosen to participate in ESA's groundbreaking "Fly!" feasibility study, which aims to systematically assess the barriers that exist in spaceflight for individuals with physical disabilities. The Fly! study is set to conclude this autumn. McFall has yet to fly in space, let alone to be assigned a slot on any upcoming mission, but that could soon change.

He now awaits his chance to launch and continues his training. *Scientific American* spoke with McFall about the process of becoming an astronaut and the unique physiological challenges uncovered in the latest feasibility study.

[*An edited transcript of the interview follows*.]

Why did you apply to participate in this study? What aspects of your background made you feel particularly suited for this project?

What was interesting about the application for this study was that there was never any guarantee of a flight to space. The notice was just for a candidate with a physical disability to participate in a feasibility study, with ESA's goal being to hopefully create an opportunity to fly someone with such a disability to space. For me, it was like, "What have I got to lose?" I didn't have going to space on my radar at all, but a friend of mine sent me a message suggesting that I look into it. I saw it as a bold and innovative opportunity, and it's commendable that ESA is the first space agency to take on such a brave initiative. In the back of my mind, I thought that if I could get selected, this would tick all the boxes for things I love doing in my life: being curious while challenging myself academically, physically and emotionally.

In terms of my background: As an amputee and surgeon, I know a lot about medicine and my disability specifically—especially what is and isn't feasible with my condition. As an athlete, I know that I'm fit and physically capable—probably an ideal person to demonstrate how capable people with physical disabilities can be. I thought I might be an ideal candidate to help answer this question.

It's somewhat surprising that we haven't had someone with a physical disability in space yet. Before doing this study, why do you think other groups hadn't tried to do this?

I don't think there is a definitive answer. If you look at the history of human spaceflight, especially in the last 20 years, the space station has been inhabited with a constant human presence since the year 2000. In the first decade [after 2000], essentially until the end of the shuttle era, the space station was still being built. We were also learning a lot about long-term human habitation in orbit. Around 2014 or 2015 we started gathering good long-term data on the effects of living in low-Earth orbit with microgravity on astronauts. Since then, the idea of whether this would be possible for someone with a physical disability has been floating around. Dave Parker, then director of human and robotic space exploration for ESA, went to all the ESA member states to get approval for selecting someone with a physical disability in 2021. It takes time, but I think the idea has been there for a while. Now that we've learned more about human spaceflight and how the body responds to prolonged microgravity, we're ready to move to the next step.

What was your immediate reaction to being selected?

When I was selected from the final few candidates, I felt privileged. I was just very proud to be selected to represent ESA and the U.K. Space Agency and also the population of people with physical disabilities. Now I have this platform and responsibility to demonstrate our capabilities.

What does the Fly! study hope to demonstrate with this feasibility testing?

There are some activities in spaceflight operations that we take for granted that able-bodied people can do because, well, why wouldn't they? Emergency procedures such as getting out of the spacecraft or medical procedures in microgravity, preflight training activities on the ground, being able to use the equipment from an ergonomic point of view—all of this has been designed around able-bodied people. If you look at those requirements and ask, "Well, astronauts are required to do this—can John with his disability and prosthesis still do that?" Some of it's like, "Well, yeah, of course I can!"

But there's no harm in asking the question anyway. It's very fair because some people don't have experience with physical disabilities, and this is where my background as a medic with a disability comes in. It's not until you pick apart the requirements for flying to space that you look at how my disability and prosthesis might impact meeting them. The goal was to find out what we need to demonstrate to prove that they can be met.

Living in the microgravity of low-Earth orbit leads to internal fluid shift and muscle atrophy, among many other effects. How exactly did the study investigate how those factors might impact you and your prosthesis specifically?

Until you actually do it, there are limited ways to replicate the conditions of low-Earth orbit. There's no substitute for being in orbit and doing it. The best we can do is come up with analog variants to simulate factors from spaceflight and then try to mitigate them as much as possible. You have to ask as many questions as you can to try to understand what the potential problems could be.

For example, yes, you would expect fluid shifts in microgravity. Generally, fluid moves from the legs up into the abdomen and thorax–so, theoretically, your lower limbs would have less volume. There will be acute and chronic fluid shifts, as well as chronic atrophy, because while you're still exercising on the station, you're not going to be able to achieve the same muscle strength and bulk as on Earth. We did analog fluid shift tests here on Earth to discern if there were any significant changes in stump volume that might affect my prosthesis fit and comfort. But we actually found there wasn't anything significant. As I said, it's impossible to replicate chronic changes without doing a longer-term bed study, in which you're laying down for weeks or months on end to simulate the muscle loss from microgravity. So we did feel it was necessary that the prosthesis I would wear have some volume adaptability in the socket. My stump is probably going to get smaller in space, so it's important to have some adjustability.

The actual spectrum of physical disabilities that this study covers is naturally limited–the testing is restricted to a single-leg amputation specifically. How much do these results generalize to the much broader spectrum of physical disabilities?

The study we've done is very specific to my disability–a single-leg amputation above the knee. You can probably extrapolate to a population of similar lower limb disabilities, but bear in mind that individual assessments would still be needed for each person.

What's interesting is when you look at a person's disability and how they would live and work in space, you need to consider where assistive devices play a role. If someone is dependent on assistive technology to undertake their tasks, as I am with my prosthesis, you have to make sure that this device works and is suitable for spaceflight.

There are several other disabilities [that merit microgravity studies], such as in the case of someone who can't use their lower limbs and is a wheelchair user. In this case, lower limb muscle atrophy or fluid shift is not really an issue because they don't walk or put weight on their lower body. They'd still need assistive devices to meet the emergency requirements at launch, but when you're up in space, getting about and doing tasks is straightforward. Yes, they may have to demonstrate that they can stabilize themselves, and we can develop technology to help. But they are actually less dependent on assistive devices in space for their physical health. We also know that astronauts in space only see a reduction in bone density in their lower limbs—so if you don't use those limbs, it doesn't matter.

There are still open questions for wheelchair users regarding bladder and bowel function and the risks associated with microgravity, which are quite interesting. Essentially, there is a lot to understand and learn about. That's what I think will be the legacy of this study.

You mentioned that in the selection process, there was no promise of being sent on a space mission and that this was purely a feasibility test. Whether you or someone else does become the first parastronaut in space, what message do you hope to convey to those who previously thought spaceflight was out of reach for people with physical disabilities?

ESA and the U.K. Space Agency are world leaders in challenging people's intuitions and perceptions of what an astronaut looks like. I don't think that human space exploration should be the only place where this happens. I hope that as a result of this, people will continue to challenge the idea of what certain professionals look like. This is another example of challenging that narrative, and I hope to spread that message.

About the Author

Max Springer is a Ph.D. candidate in applied mathematics at the University of Maryland and was a 2024 AAAS Mass Media Fellow at Scientific American.

Section 3: Living on Other Planets

NASA's Artemis Astronauts Will Help Grow Crops on the Moon—And Much More

By Robin George Andrews

In the not-too-distant future, American astronauts will once again set foot on the moon's silvery desolation. Instead of brief jaunts around the low-latitude frozen lava seas on the orb's Earth-facing hemisphere like their Apollo-era forebears, however, the moonwalkers of NASA's *Artemis III* mission will be targeting the lunar south pole—a region that holds ancient deposits of water and, just possibly, the future site of a permanent astronaut outpost. The mission will have a crew of four, but two will remain in lunar orbit while the other pair touches down on the southern polar region and scoots briefly across the surface. And as they do so, they will deploy a suite of scientific instruments to forensically examine what will then be the most important parcel of off-world real estate in the solar system.

After considering myriad proposals, NASA has now announced three gadgets chosen to accompany the *Artemis III* crew members on their voyage: The Lunar Environment Monitoring Station (LEMS) package is a remarkably precise seismometer that is designed to listen out for moonquakes and survey the lunar geological underworld. The Lunar Effects on Agricultural Flora (LEAF) instrument will attempt to grow three crops on the moon and study how they respond to the mercurial, extreme environment. And the Lunar Dielectric Analyzer (LDA) will use the flow of electric currents through the lunar soil to detect the presence of volatiles, most notably water ice.

These three instruments are not guaranteed to find their way to the lunar south pole. Additional developmental work is required to ensure each can fulfill its scientific objectives and to quadruple-check that all are compatible with *Artemis III*'s launch architecture and carefully choreographed surface excursions. But the signal NASA wishes to broadcast with this tentative selection of doodads is already loud and clear: more than a half-century after the flash and fade of Apollo, the U.S. is returning to the moon for the long haul.

"We want Artemis to be sustainable," says Noah Petro, *Artemis III*'s project scientist.

Establishing a bona fide moon base requires ascertaining several things: the risk to structures from moonquakes, the possibility of growing plants on the moon and the likelihood of finding water to use there. This trio of instruments will seek answers to those practical queries while conducting basic scientific investigations on the moon's scarcely explored far side. "We've got this great scientific story to tell," Petro says. And if all three work wonders, "we are going to be setting a precedent that other missions will have to meet."

Shaking and Quaking

Sophisticated scientific instrumentation is no stranger to the lunar surface, which now hosts a surprisingly diverse array of experiments sent there with ever increasing cadence over the past few years by multiple space agencies and spaceflight companies. But wonky landings and straight-up crashes have produced decidedly mixed results for these ventures, which all relied on automated robotic deployments.

Using astronauts to unpack and set up experimental apparatuses is far more expensive yet also has a far superior track record of success. "The added advantage of having people there is that you get a little bit more flexibility," says Ben Fernando, a seismologist at Johns Hopkins University. "People can debug things." And of course, you can ensure that the experiments are as close to their optimal locations and configurations as humanly possible–something of paramount importance to LEMS, which is one of the most precise and sensitive seismometers ever developed.

LEMS is actually a pair of seismometers, each of which will be used to detect two different types of seismic rumbles. One will be inserted into a borehole, while the other will be put into an excavated ditch. Because astronauts will place them, both are nigh guaranteed to be perfectly coupled with the ground and shielded from an excess of environmental surface noise.

It may sound absurd that digging holes is a key reason astronauts are required to deploy these seismometers. Robots have had a famously difficult time drilling into the surprisingly resistant soils of both the moon and Mars, however. Although astronauts have found this challenging, too—the Apollo moonwalkers struggled with some of their deployments—they can troubleshoot in real time in ways no robot can (yet). "Yes, it takes enormous amounts of money to put astronauts on the moon. But if they're there anyway, how hard is it for them to dig a trench?" says Paul Byrne, a planetary scientist at Washington University in St. Louis and a member of the LEMS team

Solar-powered by day and battery-powered by night, LEMS will gradually build up a richly detailed seismic picture of the understudied south pole. The experiment will beam its hard-won readings back to Earth once a month to add to preexisting data from Apollo-era seismometers at sites on the moon's near side. "If it is used as planned, this thing will last for two years on the lunar surface," Byrne says. That should be more than enough time to fill in gaps in information about the frequency of south polar moonquakes and the bulk structure of the lunar subsurface there—crucial data points for reasons of not just science but also safety.

"If you want to establish a permanent settlement on the lunar south pole, you better understand the seismic state of that environment in the long term," says Mehdi Benna, a planetary scientist at the University of Maryland, Baltimore County, and LEMS's team leader.

"I'm delighted they selected this," says Thomas Watters, a planetary scientist at the National Air and Space Museum in Washington, D.C. Apollo-era seismometers revealed not only that the moon has sporadic temblors but that some of the most intense happened around the lunar south pole. And although Earth's quakes can be far more powerful, "these things can last for hours on the moon, not just minutes," Watters says. "You've got to be prepared for that."

Quakes aren't the only things LEMS will detect. Car-sized space rocks burn up harmlessly in Earth's atmosphere, whereas they plow unimpeded into the lunar surface, making them a hazard. On the moon "impacts can happen anywhere," Fernando says–and LEMS will be able to assess the impact rate around the lunar south pole.

A Farm on the Moon

The lunar south pole's allure for human exploration comes from its nearly constant access to solar power–and also from the water ice thought to lurk in abundance within deeply shadowed craters and in the shallow subsurface. Melted and purified, that ice could be used as potable water; split into constituent hydrogen and oxygen, it could provide rocket fuel and breathable air. Yet first, scientists need to ascertain just how much H2O actually exists there to use–something that the LDA instrument will address by assessing how electric fields subtly convulse when propagating through the lunar soil.

Picking an ideal deployment spot–one that experiences both day and night, for example–could be crucial for LDA's studies. And the requisite mobility and precision are "very, very difficult for a robotic mission but probably very easy for trained astronauts," says Hideaki Miyamoto, a planetary scientist the University of Tokyo and LDA's team leader. Robots will still assist the effort, however: LDA's siting will be indirectly supported by NASA's Volatiles Investigating Polar Exploration Rover, or VIPER, which will sniff out water molecules in the south polar region after it launches later this year.

But before any lunar water is used to irrigate crops for hungry astronauts, NASA's mission planners want to ensure edible plants can even grow on the moon in the first place. That's LEAF's task. This instrument is essentially a space-age terrarium, featuring an enclosed growth chamber to nourish three crops–Wolffia (known as duckweed), Brassica rapa (related to turnip and bok choy plants) and Arabidopsis thaliana (thale-cress)–and protect them from the harsh lunar environment.

All three well-studied model plants have been flown in space before. By taking root on the moon, however, they will enter scarcely charted agricultural realms. Once LEAF has been deployed, its seeds will be pampered with water, nutrients and light in a clement atmosphere, "much like an indoor farm does on Earth," says LEAF's team leader Christine Escobar, an ecologist and vice president of Space Lab Technologies in Boulder, Colo. Cameras and various sensors will monitor their growth. Some of the quickly germinating plants will be harvested for further study by the *Artemis III* team, while others will continue to grow until the long, cold darkness of lunar night falls.

LEAF is the instrument that is most explicitly tied to the creation of a long-term presence on the lunar south pole. "Human nutrition and life support–carbon dioxide removal, oxygen production and water purification–provided by space agriculture will enable long-duration human exploration of the moon and beyond," Escobar says.

Even if LEAF's tranquil terrarium makes a giant leap in otherworldly botany, it will be but a small step toward true lunar farming, which faces myriad challenges such as lower gravity, higher radiation levels and a dearth of high-quality soil. "Lunar regolith will likely be used for plant growth facilities in established lunar bases," says Anna-Lisa Paul, a horticultural scientist at the University of Florida. She recently attempted to grow thale-cress in lunar soil obtained by the Apollo missions. Although the experiment was successful, the plants hated it; they were slow to develop and exhibited signs of stress. You must start somewhere, however, and what LEAF will tell botanists will be invaluable. "Based on what is discovered, the next step could be to help plants with specific difficulties either by engineering them to better enable them to physiologically adapt or [by] choosing crop species that are naturally better suited to dealing with that particular stress response," Paul says.

Altogether, NASA's choice of these instruments further reinforces how seriously the agency is pursuing its intentions to return humans to the moon–this time, to linger and perhaps even stay. After LEMS, LDA and LEAF have done their work, Fernando says, it'll be harder to argue against the moon as "somewhere you could, in theory, have people live for an extended period of time."

The Artemis program may have been subject to various controversies, technical challenges and budgetary overspills–but announcements like this one make the long-awaited lunar return, and NASA's ambitions to remain there, seem that much more tangible. "We're going to see humans on the moon. And that's going to start changing how we view the whole enterprise," Byrne says. "This is not going to be planting the flag and going home."

About the Author

Robin George Andrews is a volcanologist and science writer based in London. His most recent book is How To Kill An Asteroid (W.W. Norton, 2024). Follow him on X @SquigglyVolcano

Is Space the Place for Earth's Next Evolutionary Leap?

By Lee Billings

The multibillion-year story of life on Earth is defined by a handful of epochal transformations, such as the emergence of the cell, the rise of multicellular organisms and the biosphere's expansion from the primordial seas to the land and sky. Today, with life having crept into practically every possible niche on Earth, it may seem that there's nowhere else to go. But there is, of course, still one place that beckons as life's next evolutionary frontier: space. And humans are uniquely poised to propel this great transition by pushing out from our planetary cradle.

That's the case Caleb Scharf makes in his latest book, *The Giant Leap* (Basic Books, 2025). Drawing on his expertise as senior scientist for astrobiology at NASA's Ames Research Center, he argues that our modern spacefaring era is not just a matter of geopolitical competition and technological innovation but also part of a deeper, more fundamental evolutionary imperative. For the first time in Earth's history, life–with human technology as its agent–can permanently expand from one lonely planet out into the rest of the solar system. Scharf calls this new trajectory the "Dispersal" and notes it's becoming possible just as our ever growing dominion over Earth pushes the planet toward disruptive tipping points in climate change, biodiversity loss and resource use. This next great evolutionary transition, it seems, can't come too soon–because the fate of life on Earth may ultimately depend on leaving our planet behind.

Scientific American spoke with Scharf about some implications of this cosmic outlook–from the physical limits of human expansion across the solar system to the dubious quest to build settlement on Mars and the political uncertainties that could stifle the Dispersal before it even starts.

[*An edited transcript of the interview follows.*]

What was the genesis of this book?

I'd be dishonest if I didn't admit that it partly came about because I wanted to nerd out about space. But the deeper genesis was about examining the question of what it looks like, and what it means, when life moves beyond its planetary origins. There are lots of visions out there for our future in space and what happens when we've built, you know, space elevators, and so on. They can get more and more fantastical. But they usually don't tell us about the big picture; they're attempts to imagine specifics of the future, which is really difficult, and so they're probably going to get things wrong. So I wondered if, instead, we could look at what might be called the natural history of space exploration–of spaceflight as a sort of planetary phenomenon–and what that would tell us.

Let's talk about the Dispersal. What is that, exactly?

As an astrobiologist who spends my days chewing over the nature of living systems at many different levels, in both abstract and practical terms, I'm coming to this from a much broader perspective, thinking of our unfolding space age as another sort of evolutionary leap. Forget, for a minute, about the specifics of humans or even the specifics of how we're getting to space. If you think about it, gravity is glomming stuff together all across the universe to make stars and planets–and eventually more and more complex chemistry. And, at least here on Earth, life arose and evolved. And now, billions of years later, we've reached a point where our planet is throwing some sort of perverse tantrum and tossing–dispersing!–materials, machines and organisms back out into space. And I'm interested in extrapolating this process and examining how far it can go.

So the Dispersal is about what might happen to us, and all life, when it encounters scales of space and of resources that are unimaginably large. And just as you can imagine speciation happening when organisms are suddenly scattered across different terrains–like the Galápagos Islands, for instance–when life disperses beyond Earth, it can follow increasingly divergent trajectories. This means, among other things, that we're not necessarily talking about modern humans anymore in our extrapolations but whatever comes after us. It can seem kind of terrifying and awful that we might not fully recognize or identify with future "dispersed" versions of us, but those transformations aren't necessarily bad things.

That means, I guess, that whatever the Dispersal is, it's not only about rocket science–and it's not really about fantastic visions of space elevators or warp drives or the specific details of any posthuman future either. One thing I like about the book is how you're approaching this huge topic from a "first principles" perspective, initially focusing on fundamental things such as orbital mechanics that set various sorts of boundary conditions and shape the landscape of possibilities that may exist for us beyond Earth.

Yeah, this concept of boundary conditions is really important–the idea that certain phenomena can only happen within certain constraints, beyond which they can no longer take place. You need that to scope out the "landscape," as you called it. Imagine a continent where humans have never set foot, and you're trying to predict what'll happen when they do–you might say, for instance, they'll build a city, and that city will have a subway system. But if the whole continent is a waterlogged swamp, no one's going to build a subway there, and the planning for any city will have to account for the swampy conditions, and so the possibilities are different. It's the same for the solar system.

There's a chapter in the book talking about all this, looking at the range of possibilities and challenges that exist for places close in to the sun, such as Mercury, to the other extreme, far-out places such as Neptune and even further afield. The obvious difference is sunlight, which is about seven times stronger at

Mercury and more than 1,000 times fainter out at Pluto than at Earth. Usually, when an astrobiologist like me is talking about this, it's in the context of habitable zones, the physics- and chemistry-based potential for a world to have conditions such as an atmosphere, surface liquid water and other things that would allow life as we know it. But there are additional "zones" to consider if you're thinking about how technological life might disperse itself in a planetary system. They are similarly related to availability of sunlight, of energy, but also things such as how much radiation you're exposed to and how easy any destination is to reach.

It's actually really difficult to get to Mercury, for example, because it's so deep in the sun's gravity well—the amount of energy you need to get there from Earth is on par with what you need to get to Jupiter and beyond. And because Mercury is so much closer up to the sun, you can be more vulnerable to nasty flares, and so on, whereas the further you get from the sun, the less you have to worry about solar activity but the more exposed you'll be to cosmic radiation, which has its own hazards.

Accounting for all these, you might imagine a "zone of easiest exploration" that will help you understand where we're likely to go elsewhere in the solar system and how we'll get there. That's how you get clues to what the Dispersal will look like.

So, for most folks, this may be a really novel way of thinking about exploration and expansion in the solar system. But of course, for space nerds like us, lots of old, classic factions and debates pop out of this new framework.

For instance, there's the choice of prioritizing sending humans to the moon—as the U.S. and other nations are planning—versus doing crewed missions to Mars. And there's also an argument that humans shouldn't be going to planets and moons at all and should instead stick to building space stations and other sorts of artificial orbital habitats. You discuss all this at length in the book, but I had trouble discerning which route you actually prefer.

Well, in writing the book, I came to the conclusion that planets can be a real pain in the ass!

We definitely need to study Mars and the moon, and maybe some of us should even try to live there. I mean, there's all sorts of genuine reasons for doing that. But in the long term, it's far better to engineer what you really need—to create environments that place fewer stressors on life that evolved on Earth over four billion years. Even if you build fabulous habitats on the moon or Mars, you'll never have Earth-normal gravity in those places, for example.

Whether you make use of a natural object such as an asteroid or just construct an entirely artificial habitat out there, both would give you far more options than a planetary surface. You can spin your habitat to get Earth-like artificial gravity; you can engineer a lovely atmosphere that precisely fits our biological needs. You can set up seasons, choose where to orbit and have robust protection from cosmic radiation.

Relatedly, I get the sense you're not enamored with Elon Musk's dream of building cities on Mars. You even write in the book that if the rationale for Mars settlement is to safeguard humanity against existential risks, it would probably make more sense to skip Mars entirely in favor of building settlements deep underground on Earth. Why don't you find the "occupy Mars" arguments convincing?

I think it's too easy to be the sort of the space enthusiast who sits in an armchair puffing on a cigar and saying, "Oh, yes, of course we'll go conquer and colonize space." Apart from feeling discomfort at all the sociopolitical baggage and privilege associated with that attitude, I think we simply can't afford to be so blinkered and blasé—because these are unbelievably difficult and expensive things to do. And they can seem extremely disconnected from the problems that most humans face every day. So you've got to have a really sensible, sane, reasonable motivation and explanation for why anyone should want to do this, and I don't think building a city on Mars is sufficient.

Mars is a very interesting test bed for querying why we humans today, amid all our problems, should be thinking about any of this stuff. But I find today's focus on the Silicon Valley–style "let's make a backup for humanity" outlook lacking. The way it's presented reeks of a utopian "we know best" attitude—"We're going to build some glorious new society on Mars!"—when, hey, living on Mars would probably be pretty dystopian no matter what.

At the same time, yeah, no one with a big-picture view would seriously argue that life on Earth isn't subject to a variety of existential risks. So of course it makes sense to have some sort of backup—and one way to do that would indeed be to create a self-sustaining permanent settlement on Mars populated with enough people to avoid everyone becoming inbred idiots. But I don't think this can be the sole motivating factor.

So what's your preferred approach to Mars, then?

In the book I tried to examine Mars exploration by ideological camps. There's the stance we just mentioned, you know, of "let's immediately get lots of humans to Mars as an existential backup. To hell with the Martian environment or anything like that; this whole planet is just there for us to conquer and take." Then there's the pure science camp that says we really should be incredibly cautious but not entirely hands-off about sending humans or anything else to Mars, because we don't want to disrupt this near-pristine environment where there might be clues we simply can't get on Earth to the origins and fundamental nature of life. And then there's this sort of "Earth first" extreme, which says even the scientific stuff is too expensive, and space exploration as a whole is diverting attention from all the very pressing problems we have right here on Earth, so we should just stop doing it. Most debates about space policy tend to revolve around these views and usually end up in a stalemate.

I advocate for a fourth kind of approach that, in some ways, is about reinventing how we do human exploration. We know how to "connect up" and digitize a planet with sensors and satellites, and so on, because we've done that on Earth, and we're learning how to work with our machines in new, incredibly tight-knit ways. If we really put all that to work on Mars, I think there's an opportunity to do all the things we want and to learn new ways to exist.

And I guess the reason this same logic wouldn't apply to, say, the moon is that, in comparison with Mars, it offers dismal prospects for breakthroughs in our search for the origins of life.

Right. The moon is also incredibly interesting and beautiful, and it's certainly much more accessible in terms of its proximity to us. And there are resources there such as water ice that could support interplanetary exploration needs. We could also learn about processes of biological contamination there. But the moon doesn't quite tick all the boxes the same way as Mars does, yeah.

So, you know, it's not that the moon should be ignored–and it may play a pivotal role in the next several decades–but it's definitely a downgrade from Mars in my opinion.

I ask about the moon for practical reasons. As you mention, it's much easier to reach, so in some respects maybe it's like a set of training wheels for more ambitious trips to Mars, and so on. This is, of course, another resurrection of a timeless debate–some people would say it makes more sense to go to the moon first before making the bigger leap to Mars.

That is to say, it feels like, in the book, you're laying out the wonders of the solar system–"look at all these amazing worlds that await us!"–without much focus on what the path could be to get there. You're talking about the boundary conditions that exist, and the resulting zones where we might explore or even live, but less about the plausible routes by which those situations can become reality.

You mentioned evolutionary leaps earlier, and I guess that's what I'm getting at: it's not really clear to me how we're going to go from our comfortable, well-adapted lives here on Earth into, say, dwelling in city-sized space stations carved out of asteroids between Mars and Jupiter. That seems like, well—a giant leap!

That's a good observation. And it comes back to me not wanting to fall into the trap that's gotten so many people before, where someone will declare, "Clearly, *this* is the trajectory that things are going, and so *this* and *that* will absolutely happen!"

Imagine, for a moment, being back in 1968, watching three NASA astronauts on their way home to Earth after orbiting the moon for *Apollo 8*. You'd think that the future was becoming clearer, right? We were about to send more astronauts back there—to land. Maybe the Soviets would do it as well. There's going to be a lunar land rush, passenger flights to the moon and a flurry of new rockets and space stations, and then we'll be going to Mars in the 1970s. But of course, the complicated reality of human civilization got in the way, and most of that stuff didn't happen. We left that imagined trajectory for a different one—if we were ever really on it in the first place.

It's undeniable that "space" is at another inflection point today. We're rapidly approaching the point where there will be at least one rocket launch per day into orbit, which is astonishing. There are now around 10,000 space-oriented companies around the world, which definitely wasn't the case 10 years ago. And I think it's fair to say even the growth in the value of Earth data obtained from space has shot up. So all the curves seem to be following this exponential upward slope. That's not a guarantee it keeps going. Regression is possible. Or maybe just a flattening of the curves into a plateau might happen—which would still be interesting because then the question would be: Is there still something in the future that could occur to create more exponential growth?

I don't know if that gets to your question exactly, but I feel there's sufficient evidence that something new is happening right now that we should pay attention to–and it may presage the beginnings of the Dispersal. The point is: I don't think it's likely that we'll just repeat history, right? There will be surprises. It's no longer as simple as it was in the Apollo era, when you could really see most everything through the lens of "the U.S. versus the Soviets" in space.

The situation we have today is a much richer, more complicated set of motivations, actors and capabilities. So it becomes more relevant to consider the ultimate end points in those vast scales and resources of the solar system and what those limits might mean–rather than the limits of earthly thinking about what will happen next week.

Overall, it seems you're presenting a pretty optimistic big picture of where we're going from here. But to zoom in on smaller details for a moment, you're also saying this while being furloughed from your NASA work because of the latest U.S. government shutdown while the space agency is facing steep budget cuts and workforce reductions–things that I'd imagine someone like you would be pessimistic about. How do you reconcile this?

Let me start by saying that finding the bigger perspective always helps in times of uncertainty! In that context, I think the Dispersal is a hugely positive idea, with relevance no matter what the current earthly circumstances are. What life often does when it disperses is find opportunities to do better. The human species is no different. And the universe seems to be tilted towards making that happen. So, to some degree, I think it's out of any one group's control.

Space exploration is happening; there's just a critical mass of financial interests, of people's pet interests, of individuals with resources who are interested in this, of countries that still see the enormous value in having access to space for all sorts of reasons–economic reasons, security reasons or maybe just for national pride. With all these players, I think we're crossing a threshold that we didn't quite get to in the 1960s and 1970s. And having so many players in the mix also means that who gets to do what first is an open question.

That is relevant to your point about NASA–I'm speaking personally here and not for the agency in any way. It's irrefutable that the pioneering efforts of NASA have been key for getting space exploration to where it is today. We've learned that when you solve the hard problems of space with long-term investments in science, engineering and people, it paves the way for others to further innovate. That's great because the hard problems will keep coming. We just need to figure out how to keep this special recipe working.

Where I'm not optimistic is the idea that we'll get together as a species and draw up some unified master plan for humanity and space. Forget it. That's not happening, right? But I think that's okay. What we're going to see are multiple ideas and efforts and innovations all at once at a level that hasn't existed ever before. And in retrospect, it makes a lot of sense that it's happening like this rather than how it looked like it might for most of the 20th century. Throughout human history, there have been moments where advances just "come together," whether it was the printing press or mass transport or telecommunications or computing and the Internet. These are invariably fueled by science, as well as by competing interests in realms of economic or commercial opportunity, driving investments in multiple places.

I feel like that's where we're at now with space. And that, to me, is new and pretty amazing.

About the Author

Lee Billings is a science journalist specializing in astronomy, physics, planetary science, and spaceflight and is senior desk editor for physical science at Scientific American. *He is author of a critically acclaimed book,* Five Billion Years of

Solitude: The Search for Life Among the Stars, *which in 2014 won a Science Communication Award from the American Institute of Physics. In addition to his work for* Scientific American, *Billings's writing has appeared in the* New York Times, *the* Wall Street Journal, *the* Boston Globe, Wired, New Scientist, Popular Science *and many other publications. Billings joined Scientific American in 2014 and previously worked as a staff editor at SEED magazine. He holds a B.A. in journalism from the University of Minnesota.*

Mars Can Wait. Questions Surround Settlements on Other Worlds

By Mikko M. Puumala, Oskari Sivula & Kirsi Lehto

As ever-deepening turmoil engulfs Earth, daydreaming about moving to Mars might provide a pleasant break from our everyday predicaments. It is entirely understandable–and human–to grasp onto promises of a better life in a faraway place. But when Martian daydreams, in particular, turn into reality, the picture becomes less pleasant. What promise could a barren, hostile planet like Mars hold? As far as the solar system is concerned, we already inhabit a paradise.

Nevertheless, Mars is on the menu. NASA's proposed Artemis mission ends with people planting flags on Martian soil in coming decades. China plans a sample return mission to Mars, and India plans to send another orbiter there in 2024. Even Earth's newest space billionaire, Elon Musk, has joked about spending his last years on Mars, apparently intending to make humans a multiplanetary species.

The wildest plans for Mars–at the far edges of plausibility–include settling a million people permanently on another planet. Such an endeavor, like any mission that involves sending people to outer space, would be extremely risky and expensive. Some visions to take a large group of humans to stay permanently on the Martian surface would require rockets transporting 100 metric tons of cargo or 150 passengers at a time to land directly onto the Martian surface. To reach a million inhabitants of the Red Planet within a century would require approximately 7,000 passenger ship trips as well as more than 50,000 food cargo flights (not to mention the transport flights for the machinery, components and other materials), feasible only during the launch window that opens every two years. Even with this excessive expenditure, life would remain very restricted and risky for Mars immigrants. Thus, you'd need a very good justification for this kind of large-scale settlement. After all, it is not merely an engineering challenge but also an ethical one.

The rapidly growing space ethics literature discusses several reasons for space expansionism, for example, new scientific knowledge and discovery, long-term survival of humanity, economic benefits, inspiration and adventure. Do any of these justify the costs, risks and dangers involved in establishing a permanent Martian settlement? Frankly, no. While most of them fail for various grounds, the only shoe that fits is too weak to justify such an enterprise.

Studying Mars IRL may reveal important scientific discoveries, such as extinct or extant life on Mars. Thus, science provides a great reason to go to Mars–just not for a permanent settlement. A smaller outpost would be enough for most scientific inquiry. Furthermore, larger-scale settlement activities directly conflict with some scientific goals. Large human populations, through habitation and excavation, could contaminate the objects of studies and interfere with research.

At face value, the long-term survival of humanity seems to provide a solid and noble cause for building permanent settlements on Mars. However, for a Mars settlement to truly mitigate extinction risks it must be adequately self-sufficient. This is unlikely to be achieved any time soon, and we may not have the time to wait. Instead, investments in global food security, meteor or comet deflection, pandemic preparedness and global peace appear far more cost-effective than building a settlement off-world. Additionally, some risks may follow us to Mars, such as rogue artificial intelligence, meaning that a settlement on Mars does not lower the total risk of extinction that much. Therefore, while in the long term safeguarding humanity may provide a good reason to settle other planets, it does not give us an urgent one.

The economic promise of Mars also seems tempting, but it may prove to be specious. For now, interplanetary travel and operating in deep space are just too expensive. Most economic opportunities are better cashed out closer to Earth. For example, it is likely far more cost-effective to mine the moon or near-earth asteroids rather than Mars or the asteroid belt. The same probably applies to tourism or space manufacturing. Moreover, industries on Mars may jeopardize scientific goals. Hence, if we want both scientific and economic benefits of Mars, the science should come first and business later.

Settling Mars could also provide inspiration for both settlers and the large majority safe on Earth. Even so, it is not clear that it would be inspirational enough to be worth it. One can of course tell fanciful stories about how settling Mars helps us avoid societal stagnation and provide new spiritual insights and fruitful political and philosophical ideas, but it sounds a lot like wishful thinking or an act of faith. Also, the sheer achievement of going to Mars could prove inspiring, but it is not clear that we need a million people there for that kind of inspiration; the first four or so pairs of boots on Mars would likely do the trick. Looking to the moon landings, the first ones captured great attention, but subsequent Apollo mission interest soon faded, with daily quiz shows garnering higher ratings. The same could happen with Mars.

Finally, one obvious reason for going to Mars is the sheer adventure of it.Indeed, extraordinary adventure and thrills would await those brave individuals who settle Mars. And unlike the other reasons, adventure does not become redundant after a certain point. There can always be more adventure for more people, while the other reasons can be fulfilled with less risky and expensive endeavors like a small science outpost. This makes adventure in one sense the strongest reason for establishing a million-person society on Mars. Of course, it is appropriate to question whether the gargantuan effort of building a permanent settlement on the Red Planet can be justified by such a frivolous reason as adventure. In this sense, the strongest reason for settling Mars is also the weakest.

We can pursue the other goals with far less risk and expense than a Mars settlement entails. NASA has produced multiple small exploration mission designs. None have been pursued, in light of the high cost of safely sending humans to Mars. However, crewed missions, and maybe a station either in Mars orbit or the surface, are again being planned to continue the Artemis program. At the forefront of current space technology, that is far more realistic than sending a million people to Mars.

Dreaming about Mars can be valuable and has sparked discussion and research in many fields. Yet, perhaps for the time being it should remain only a dream.

About the Authors

Mikko M. Puumala is a postdoc researcher in philosophy at the University of Turku, Finland.

Oskari Sivula is a doctoral researcher in philosophy at the University of Turku, Finland.

Kirsi Lehto is an astrobiologist and a docent at the University of Turku, Finland.

Can We Even Have Babies in Space? Why We're Not Ready for Life Off-Planet

By Clara Moskowitz

Star Trek makes living in space look great: it depicts a utopian future without hunger or climate devastation and with technology that can zoom you across the galaxy and produce holographic playgrounds for relaxing in your free time. (Never mind that pesky war with the Klingons.) But the reality of space settlements would likely involve deprivation, harsh conditions and difficult interactions among a small, isolated group of people. Behavioral ecologist Kelly Weinersmith and her cartoonist husband Zach Weinersmith set out to research the future of space settlements and found, to their dismay, that the prospect looked miserable.

Space is inhospitable: its radiation and lack of gravity wreak havoc on the body; the legal situation is murky at best; and there's the looming disaster of trying to reproduce beyond Earth. The Weinersmiths discuss these risks and more in their new book, *A City on Mars* (Penguin Random House, 2023). Their laugh-out-loud-funny descriptions highlight a sobering truth: humanity isn't ready to spread among the solar system anytime soon.

The Weinersmiths spoke to *Scientific American* about space war risks, giving birth beyond Earth and the legality of space cannibalism.

[*An edited transcript of the conversation follows*.]

You started off thinking very differently about living in space than you do now. How did that happen?

KELLY WEINERSMITH: That's totally right. I'm a sci-fi geek, and I've always thought that living in a space settlement would be really awesome. We thought, this is coming soon, and we're going to write a guide for what it's going to be like as we start making these settlements in the next years or decades. And then, you know, every chapter we researched, we were like, "Oh, crud. We [humans] don't know anything about this." And at the end, we just thought, not only can we not do it safely yet, but it could create a lot more existential risks down here on Earth. And there are also the ethical implications of what essentially sounds to us like experimental research on babies if you just start having kids on Mars. Those all seemed bad.

As you learned more and more about what living in space might involve, you discovered all these new hurdles and potential deal-breakers. What are the biggest things standing in our way?

ZACH WEINERSMITH: One thing is reproduction [in space], about which we know nothing. That's foremost for the simple reason that it's obviously massively unethical not to have that information before you start this. And then there's some stuff that's merely hard and then some stuff that's maybe unsolvable. Ecosystem creation is extremely intricate and complicated. The best example we have is probably Biosphere 2, which had eight people who were starving and angry at each other [after living there for two years in a contained desert ecosystem in Arizona]. So if you want a million-person greenhouse on Mars, it's like a greenhouse the size of Singapore. And so it's a project that's just going to take an enormous amount of time to get answers on, and nobody is spending at scale on it. And then another big issue, I would say, is that you could get a scramble situation for turf in space. You know, conflict happens, and the good turf is actually quite limited. That's a scary possibility. We argue that there needs to be some kind of regulation of how the process works to avoid conflict.

Going back to the question of having babies in space: Are there reasons to think that it's going to be very hard to sustain a pregnancy and give birth in microgravity or on Mars or the moon?

KELLY WEINERSMITH: Yeah, I think so. The radiation in space, for example, messes up gametes, and for the adults that are walking around, that could give you problems down the line—especially for women, because we're born with our gametes, and so they're going to be acquiring radiation throughout the course of our life. And then we need to have kids, and then those kids need to have kids, and so everything needs to be okay for generations. And we just do not know enough about how space radiation impacts bodies.

And then the other problem is: we don't really know how partial gravity is going to impact human bodies. We know that the microgravity you experience on the International Space Station is definitely associated with bone loss. On a six-month journey, the astronauts that went up there lost 1.5 percent of their bone mineral density per month. If you're living up there—even if you're only losing part of that—by the time you're reproductive age and you're ready to have a kid, you don't want to be crossing your fingers hoping that your hips don't shatter when you go into labor.

You also highlight space law as a problem that gets swept under the rug but really needs to be dealt with. In fact, you say law is a problem "bigger than science or technology" when it comes to settling in space—because essentially it's currently illegal to claim specific territory in space, right?

ZACH WEINERSMITH: This is the big, giant thing nobody's talking about. Space advocates, many of them, just say, "Oh, you know, when we can finally start our settlement on Mars, the international community will just be in awe of our amazingness, and they'll think, 'We couldn't possibly constrain them.'" One famous book about settling Mars, by Robert Zubrin, is *The Case for Mars*. It's 400 pages long but does not mention the United Nations Outer Space Treaty, which is the main document governing space, at all.

KELLY WEINERSMITH: A lot of people are hoping that when the time comes, this problem will just go away. Some people think that when the time comes, the U.S. government will be willing to just pull out of this treaty that's been widely ratified for half a century.

ZACH WEINERSMITH: There are also people who think that when there is something valuable to do in space, people—whether it's Elon Musk or the U.S. at large—will just do whatever it takes to go get the stuff because economics trumps geopolitics. I think there's this idea that the moment there's cash money to be made on the moon, none of this [legislation] matters. And we disagree.

A lot of people talk about settling space as a way to make us safer—a plan B in case we accidentally destroy human civilization on Earth. But you write that settling space may actually make us less safe. How does that work?

ZACH WEINERSMITH: If you have a world where there's just more stuff going at higher speed around the solar system, and it's controlled by more players, then you're just in a world of higher danger. [If an object in space hits another] at three kilometers per second, [its] kinetic energy is equivalent to the object being made out of TNT if it impacts , right? And a world with a million tons of metal controlled by private actors in low-Earth orbit is one that imperils Earth below. I don't see how that's avoidable.

In addition, you know, we don't believe there's big value on the moon, but space agencies and governments talk about it. So far there has not been a big scramble on the moon, but now we're getting to a world where that [relative lack of interest] might not be the case. And that's scary because the major players are powerful, highly militarized nations, and they all have nuclear weapons.

And the last thing is that there tends to be this assumption that going multiplanetary necessarily decreases existential risk for humanity. Having two [homes] is better than one. But there are reasons to think that in the longer-term future, if you ever got to a point where you could have war between planets, it could be extraordinarily dangerous. This is because we would be down gravity wells from each other, which not only means that you would get free "boom" from throwing objects but also that you could, in principle, use biological weapons without blowback.

For many people the biggest appeal of living in space is this idea that life will just be better. There will be no sexism or racism; we'll leave behind all the social problems we have here on Earth. And you point out that we're probably going to just take all these problems with us, and they might even be exacerbated. Why do you think people assume that space will be utopian?

ZACH WEINERSMITH: It's kind of like this perfect nowhere, you know, this other place where we can just kind of cut ties. The thing that should make you most suspicious is that different groups have nonoverlapping utopias that they hope will be achieved in space. A very big thread is the libertarian frontier—we're going to go to space and become sort of manly, rugged tough guys, and we'll leave all this wimpy, bureaucratic, socialist stuff behind. But then there are people who are like, we'll have communes in space. A big name in theorizing about rotating space stations was Gerard K. O'Neill, who was famous in the 1970s, and a big sell for him with this project was that you could try out new forms of government in these little island stations, as in, "We can try it all and see who's right." So utopianism has been there since the beginning. It continues now. And there's just not good evidence for it.

Okay, here's a serious question: How did you come to have an actual section of the book dedicated to space cannibalism?

KELLY WEINERSMITH: [Laughing] Okay, so Zach was like, "Why don't we have a section on the legality of space cannibalism?" And at first, I was like, "No! This is a serious book. We can make some jokes, but we're not going to have a whole section on cannibalism!" And then I read this book by Erik Seedhouse about Mars. And he mentions cannibalism a couple of times. It has this very detailed section about how you can 3-D print implements to cut the people up and who should get cut up first.

In the margins of the book, I wrote, "WTF?!" At that point, I thought, okay, I can see where this could go.

ZACH WEINERSMITH: My favorite part of the Seedhouse book was that there was literally a picture of astronauts with the caption "Is it wrong to waste such a neatly packaged meal?" And then we found this paper on survival homicide in the context of space. It was this perfect review paper on whether you can murder someone to survive in space.

KELLY WEINERSMITH: Then I was like, "Okay, you are cleared to start researching space cannibalism."

Final question: After taking this journey and learning everything that you have, do you ultimately think that we will ever live in space? And do you think we should?

KELLY WEINERSMITH: I still think it would be really cool if humans lived in space. I still love the idea of people waking up on the moon and maybe opening up their little portal and looking out on Earth and enjoying that view. But I don't think it's going to happen in my lifetime. And I don't want it to happen in my lifetime, because I'd love to see us do the research first to make sure everything is safe–you know, have a research station on the moon for a couple decades where we work out, for instance, "Are rodents okay reproducing in space?" and "Can we make a closed ecosystem where the parts don't break for more than two years, so we know that people on Mars will be okay?" And I'd like us to very slowly figure out rules for how to extract and use resources and who's allowed to go where. All this stuff is going to take a long time. But I don't think humans will ever give up the dream of living in space and being multiplanetary, and I think that's great. I just hope we do it slowly.

ZACH WEINERSMITH: Eventually, hopefully, we will go to Mars en masse just because it's awesome. It's an aesthetic choice we can make when we are an extremely rich and very advanced and very safe civilization. It's like Star Trek; you're exploring because exploring is fun. It's not going to make us rich; it's not going to make us utopian communards or save the environment or any of the other stuff. It's just cool.

About the Author

Clara Moskowitz is chief of reporters at Scientific American, *where she covers astronomy, space, physics and mathematics. She has been at* Scientific American *for more than a decade; previously she worked at Space.com. Moskowitz has reported live from rocket launches, space shuttle liftoffs and landings, suborbital spaceflight training, mountaintop observatories, and more. She has a bachelor's degree in astronomy and physics from Wesleyan University and a graduate degree in science communication from the University of California, Santa Cruz.*

Are We Ready for Death in Space?

By Peter Cummings

In 2012 NASA stealthily slipped a morgue into orbit.

No press release. No fanfare. Just a sealed, soft-sided pouch tucked in a cargo shipment to the International Space Station (ISS) alongside freeze-dried meals and scientific gear. Officially, it was called the Human Remains Containment Unit (HRCU). To the untrained eye it looked like a shipping bag for frozen cargo. But to NASA it marked something far more sobering: a major advance in preparing for death beyond Earth.

As a kid, I obsessed over how astronauts went to the bathroom in zero gravity. Now, decades later, as a forensic pathologist and a perennial applicant to NASA's astronaut corps, I find myself fixated on a darker, more haunting question:

What would happen if an astronaut died out there? Would they be brought home, or would they be left behind? If they expired on some other world, would that be their final resting place? If they passed away on a spacecraft or space station, would their remains be cast off into orbit—or sent on an escape-velocity voyage to the interstellar void?

NASA, it turns out, has begun working out most of these answers. And none too soon. Because the question itself is no longer *if* someone will die in space—but *when*.

A Graying Corps

No astronaut has ever died of natural causes off-world. In 1971 the three-man crew of the Soviet *Soyuz 11* mission asphyxiated in space when their spacecraft depressurized shortly before its automated atmospheric reentry—but their deaths were only discovered once the spacecraft landed on Earth. Similarly, every U.S. spaceflight fatality to date has occurred within Earth's atmosphere—under gravity, oxygen and a clear national jurisdiction. That matters, because it means every spaceflight mortality has played out in familiar territory.

But planned missions are getting longer, with destinations beyond low-Earth orbit. And NASA's astronaut corps is getting older. The average age now hovers around 50—an age bracket where natural death becomes statistically relevant, even for clean-living fitness buffs. Death in space is no longer a thought experiment. It's a probability curve—and NASA knows it.

In response, the agency is making subtle but decisive moves. The most recent astronaut selection cycle was extended—not only to boost intake but also to attract younger crew members capable of handling future long-duration missions.

NASA's Space Morgue

If someone were to die aboard the ISS today, their body would be placed in the HRCU, which would then be sealed and secured in a nonpressurized area to await eventual return to Earth.

The HRCU itself is a modified version of a military-grade body bag designed to store human remains in hazardous environments. It integrates with refrigeration systems already aboard the ISS to slow decomposition and includes odor-control filters and moisture-absorbent linings, as well as reversed zippers for respectful access at the head. There are straps to secure the body in a seat for return, and patches for name tags and national flags.

Cadaver tests conducted in 2019 at Sam Houston State University have proved the system durable. Some versions held for over 40 days before decomposition breached the barrier. NASA even drop-tested the bag from 19 feet to simulate a hard landing.

But it's never been used in space. And since no one yet knows how a body decomposes in true microgravity (or, for that matter, on the moon), no one can really say whether the HRCU would preserve tissue well enough for a forensic autopsy.

This is a troubling knowledge gap, because in space, a death isn't just a tragic loss—it's also a vital data point. Was an astronaut's demise from a fluke of their physiology, or an unavoidable stroke of cosmic bad luck—or was it instead a consequence of flaws in a space habitat's myriad systems that might be found and fixed? Future lives may depend on understanding what went wrong, via a proper postmortem investigation.

But there's no medical examiner in orbit. So NASA trains its crews in something called the In-Mission Forensic Sample Collection protocol. The space agency's astronauts may avoid talking about it, but they all have it memorized: Document everything, ideally with real-time guidance from NASA flight surgeons. Photograph the body. Collect blood and vitreous fluid, as well as hair and tissue samples. Only then can the remains be stowed in the HRCU.

NASA has also prepared for death outside the station—on spacewalks, the moon or deep space missions. If a crew member perishes in vacuum but their remains are retrieved, the body is wrapped in a specially designed space shroud.

The goal isn't just a technical matter of preventing contamination. It's psychological, too, as a way of preserving dignity. Of all the "firsts" any space agency hopes to achieve, the first-ever human corpse drifting into frame on a satellite feed is not among them.

If a burial must occur—in lunar regolith or by jettisoning into solar orbit—the body will be dutifully tracked and cataloged, treated forevermore as a hallowed artifact of space history.

Such gestures are also of relevance to NASA's plans for off-world mourning; grief and memorial protocols are now part of official crew training. If a death occurs, surviving astronauts are tasked with holding a simple ceremony to honor the fallen—then to move on with their mission.

Uncharted Realms

So far we've only covered the "easy" questions. NASA and others are still grappling with harder ones.

Consider the issue of authority over a death and mortal remains. On the ISS, it's simple: the deceased astronaut's home country retains jurisdiction. But that clarity fades as destinations grow more distant and the voyages more diverse: What really happens on space-agency missions to the moon, or to Mars? How might rules change for commercial or multinational spaceflights—or, for that matter, the private space stations and interplanetary settlements that are envisioned by Elon Musk, Jeff Bezos and other tech multibillionaires?

NASA and its partners have started drafting frameworks, like the Artemis Accords—agreements signed by more than 50 nations to govern behavior in space. But even those don't address many intimate details of death.

What happens, for instance, if foul play is suspected?

The Outer Space Treaty, a legal document drafted in 1967 under the United Nations that is humanity's foundational set of rules for orbit and beyond, doesn't say.

Of course, not everything can be planned for in advance. And NASA has done an extraordinary job of keeping astronauts in orbit alive. But as more people venture into space, and as the frontier stretches to longer voyages and farther destinations, it becomes a statistical certainty that sooner or later someone won't come home.

When that happens, it won't just be a tragedy. It will be a test. A test of our systems, our ethics and our ability to adapt to a new dimension of mortality. To some, NASA's preparations for astronautical death may seem merely morbid, even silly—but that couldn't be further from the truth.

Space won't care of course, whenever it claims more lives. But we will. And rising to that grim occasion with reverence, rigor and grace will define not just policy out in the great beyond—but what it means to be human there, too.

About the Author

Peter Cummings is a forensic pathologist and neuropathologist who explores what happens in the brain at the threshold between life and death. His research focuses on how the human mind and brain adapt—and sometimes transform—when pushed to their absolute limits. He is on Substack and Instagram.

Section 4: Alien Lifeforms

Human Missions to Mars Must Search for Alien Life, New Report Finds

By Lee Billings

The best reason to send humans to Mars isn't for guts or glory—or the construction of colonies to safeguard against existential Earth-bound risks. Instead it's to answer a single, simple question: Is or has there ever been life on Mars?

That's the upshot of a new report published on Tuesday by the U.S. National Academies of Sciences, Engineering, and Medicine that presents an ambitious, science-centric vision for human missions to the Red Planet—with the search for alien life as their guiding star.

"When our astronauts set foot on Mars, it will be one of humanity's greatest milestones," says Dava Newman, an aerospace engineer and former director of the MIT Media Lab, who co-chaired the committee behind the report. "And finding extant or extinct life on Mars will be the discovery that defines the next century."

The report attempts to bridge the gaps between NASA's science and its human spaceflight program in pursuit of a common goal, says report co-chair Lindy Elkins-Tanton—a planetary scientist who helms the University of California, Berkeley's Space Sciences Laboratory, as well as NASA's Psyche mission. "Learning how to blend these different disciplines is critical to our future as an interplanetary species," she says.

The report lays out an additional 10 science objectives beyond the primary search for life and ranks four potential crewed campaigns, each composed of three sequential missions.

The highest-ranking campaign suggests targeting an as-yet-unselected, geologically diverse 100-kilometer-wide "exploration zone" rich with near-surface glacial ice, where signs of past or present life might be found. That project would involve astronauts initially staying on Mars for 30 sols (Martian days). This period would then be followed by an uncrewed cargo delivery and, finally, a 300-sol-long crewed mission.

The other campaigns would be slightly smaller in scope but audacious nonetheless. Two would involve building and operating drilling rigs on Mars, with one campaign proposing to drill as far down as five kilometers to reach subsurface regions where potentially life-bearing liquid water might exist. The lowest-ranked campaign deviates from the others in that it would see astronauts mount a series of shorter surface forays of 30 sols each at three separate sites across the planet.

All the campaigns propose leveraging "human-agent teaming" in the form of advanced robotics and software. And all include a "Mars surface laboratory" for immediate studies of samples–some of which would be later returned to Earth for deeper analysis.

Such "agents" might range from small autonomous devices to humanoid robots, says report committee member and former NASA astronaut Jim Pawelczyk, now a physiologist at Pennsylvania State University. "Their exact form will be determined by specific requirements, advances in hardware and artificial intelligence. That's why it's important to set the scientific objectives early; they drive subsequent technology development," he says.

Yet, despite the 240-page report's encyclopedic descriptions of each campaign, per its NASA-directed statement of task, the committee has left several crucial issues to be addressed by other, future studies. The report doesn't, for instance, identify specific exploration zones or lay out protocols for maintaining crew health and safety. Nor does it offer any preferred approach for "planetary protection," the term for safeguarding against biological cross-contamination between Earth and Mars. (Present planetary protection guidelines would, in fact, prohibit crewed landings anywhere on Mars where liquid water is known to exist.)

These ambiguities are unlikely to be linked solely to the report's strict focus on science, according to Jim Green, a former chief scientist at NASA and former leader of the agency's planetary science division, who was not involved in the work. NASA's budget is a political football, subject to radical shifts as presidents and congressional majorities change. The Trump administration, for instance, has proposed abandoning a NASA-led multibillion-dollar effort to retrieve samples that were already gathered by the agency's Perseverance rover on Mars. "Due to the slowdown of the Mars robotic exploration program, we just don't know enough about Mars to select one exploration zone as originally planned," Green says.

The report also largely avoids the question of how any of its proposals would actually get done. It acknowledges NASA's preexisting "Moon to Mars strategy"–agency shorthand for the Artemis program to return astronauts to the lunar surface as a precursor for human voyages to the Red Planet–but is agnostic about the timing for future Mars missions and the specific types of rocketry and spacecraft required to achieve them.

"Our frankly gargantuan task was to decide what science should be done by humans–and done best by humans," Newman says. "There are going to be so many discoveries and advancements in technology that will be needed for these missions; if we constrained ourselves to the way we can do things now, we wouldn't be designing the right campaigns for our future," she adds, noting that the report doesn't try to outline how to do everything from a technological standpoint.

What is clear, Elkins-Tanton says, is that the moon remains NASA's next astronautical target, and putting boots on Mars remains firmly in the future. "We don't just go to Mars tomorrow," she says.

About the Author

Lee Billings is a science journalist specializing in astronomy, physics, planetary science, and spaceflight and is senior desk editor for physical science at Scientific American. *He is author of a critically acclaimed book,* Five Billion Years of Solitude: The Search for Life Among the Stars, *which in 2014 won a Science Communication Award from the American Institute of Physics. In addition to his work for Scientific American, Billings's writing has appeared in the* New York Times, *the* Wall Street Journal, *the* Boston Globe, Wired, New Scientist, Popular Science *and many other publications. Billings joined Scientific American in 2014 and previously worked as a staff editor at* SEED *magazine. He holds a B.A. in journalism from the University of Minnesota.*

The Search for Extraterrestrial Life Is a Roller Coaster of Hope and Disappointment

By Sarah Scoles

In the late 1800s Italian astronomer Giovanni Schiaparelli pointed a telescope at Mars and saw something curious: linear features that he called canali, meaning "channels" or "grooves." A mistranslation of that word helped lead to a widespread belief that the planet closest to Earth hosted a civilization.

American astronomer Percival Lowell took Schiaparelli's observations and ran with them. He became obsessed with the Martian markings, which he interpreted as evidence of a sophisticated network of water-transportation channels. "That Mars is inhabited by beings of some sort or other we may consider as certain as it is uncertain what those beings may be," Lowell wrote in his 1906 book Mars and Its Canals.

It sounds ludicrous now, but it wasn't back then. At the time, ideas about life were evolving rapidly, says David Baron, author of the new book *The Martians: The True Story of an Alien Craze That Captured Turn-of-the-Century America*. In 1858 Charles Darwin published his theory of natural selection. One year later German scientists Robert Wilhelm Bunsen and Gustav Robert Kirchhoff invented the spectroscope, which they and others used to analyze the chemical signatures in light from the sun and the planets. These studies revealed that other worlds are made of the same elemental constituents as Earth. If life evolves by a natural process, and all planets form in similar ways, why wouldn't life take hold on the Red Planet, too?

More than 100 years later scientists searching for extraterrestrial life are guided by the same reasoning: The universe is vast, and it's all made of the same basic stuff we are, so why wouldn't there be life elsewhere? Yet the evidence for intelligent life beyond

Earth has taken several turns. In fact, the only constant has been hope: the desire that many people have to prove we are not alone. The question of extraterrestrial life's existence isn't just a neutral scientific debate–it matters to humans, including the humans searching for that life. And our optimism that we'll find it has tended to flip on and off.

The idea that Mars is home to canal-digging civilizations began to lose its sparkle in 1909, when French astronomer Eugène Antoniadi observed the Red Planet during one of its biannual close approaches. The lines, he found with a better telescope and a more intimate view, were an optical illusion. Those data didn't convince Lowell, and it didn't put the theory to rest–in 1916 Scientific American managing editor Waldemar Kaempffert was still convinced the canals were real. Nevertheless, belief in advanced life on Mars faded in the following decades. When the Mariner 4 spacecraft flew by Mars in 1965, relaying images of a dry and desolate world, the Martian hypothesis died for good.

And the signs weren't promising for extraterrestrials elsewhere, either. In 1950 physicist Enrico Fermi had pointed out what he called the "Great Silence": If life is likely to be plentiful, then where is everybody? The fact that humanity hadn't heard from other intelligent beings became known as the Fermi paradox. Maybe life is common, but advanced life is rare, scientists suggested. Or perhaps other civilizations arise often and then destroy themselves, as humanity seemed newly capable of doing after the invention of the atomic bomb in 1945.

Astronomers began a more systematic study of the question. In 1960 Cornell University researcher Frank Drake started Project Ozma, which used a radio telescope to scan for broadcasts from two distant star systems. In 1977 astronomers caught a batch of radio waves that blasted out for 72 seconds, looking more like a hugely powerful cosmic radio station than something natural. They called it the WOW! Signal and got excited. But the same transmission was never heard again. So far the search for extraterrestrial intelligence (SETI) has not found convincing evidence of broadcasting aliens.

Yet lately there are new reasons to hope. In 1992 astronomers Aleksander Wolszczan and Dale Frail discovered two rocky worlds circling a dense, rotating star called a pulsar. Although those planets are bombarded with too much radiation to be habitable, more exoplanet discoveries trickled in through the 2000s. Then the Kepler space mission launched in 2009. It revealed thousands of worlds beyond this one, with more than 5,900 total confirmed as of publication time. "Planets became the rule, not the exception," says Nathalie Cabrol, director of the Carl Sagan Center for the Study of Life in the Universe at the SETI Institute.

This wealth of worlds once again changed the calculus on the likelihood of life beyond Earth. Back in 1961 Drake developed a formula to calculate the odds of communicating with extraterrestrial civilizations. It factored in the rate of star formation, the fraction of stars with planets, the fraction of those that are habitable, the proportion of habitable planets that actually develop life, the proportion of that life that becomes intelligent, the fraction of civilizations that develop communications technology, and the length of time they are likely to be transmitting. Most of those variables were unknown at the time–and still are–but the exoplanet boom helped to narrow down the second variable, and it's making headway on the third. We now have a much better idea of how many stars host planets, and it's at least most of them.

We still don't know how life started here on Earth, so we don't know how it might happen elsewhere. And we don't know how likely advanced civilizations are to destroy themselves–a pressing question for reasons beyond SETI. But we do now know that primitive life can thrive in profoundly inhospitable conditions, and that means that microbial aliens may be a lot easier to find than intelligent ones.

In 1966 ecologist Thomas Brock discovered the first extremophile, Thermus aquaticus, living in the hot pools of Yellowstone. Since then, scientists have found microscopic organisms in hydrothermal vents at the bottom of the ocean and in toxic mine waste, in the interiors of rocks and in radioactive water. Just because a planet looks barren doesn't necessarily mean that it is. There is good reason to think primitive life could survive in the buried oceans of Jupiter's moon Europa and the geysers of Enceladus, a moon around Saturn. There might even be microbes in the pools of meltwater under the ice caps of Mars. More than a century after Percival Lowell and his illusory Martian civilization, science has given us plenty of reason to think we're not alone, even if aliens turn out to be single-celled organisms rather than canal-building architects.

About the Author

Sarah Scoles is a Colorado-based science journalist and a contributing editor at Scientific American. Her newest book is Countdown: The Blinding Future of Nuclear Weapons (Bold Type Books, 2024).

Scientists Discover Earth Life inside an Asteroid Sample

By Sharmila Kuthunur

In November 2022 Matthew Genge was peering through a scanning electron microscope at a millimeter-sized speck of the asteroid Ryugu when he noticed something was off. A minuscule yet unmistakable rod-shaped tendril of organic matter previously unseen clung to the surface. "I thought, 'Well, that's strange,'" Genge recalls. "Then I found another and another."

For a brief time, he and his colleagues mused that they might have just made the most epochal find in human history–the discovery of alien life, imported to Earth in a few grams of material retrieved from a space rock. The Japan Aerospace Exploration Agency (JAXA) mission Hayabusa2 had snagged the samples in 2019 and delivered them to a touchdown site in remote Australia in an airtight capsule the following year. JAXA scientists then cataloged individual particles using sterilized tools in state-of-the-art clean rooms and shipped them to researchers worldwide–Genge's group included–in nitrogen-filled, sealed containers.

But if the diminutive strands were aliens, they sure looked and behaved a lot like hungry earthly microbes, gorging themselves on nutrients in the tiny fleck of Ryugu to swell their numbers 10-fold before dying off under a bombardment of scanning electron microscope measurements by the curious scientists. Watching the boom-and-bust cycle, Genge and his colleagues realized that the rods were almost certainly invaders from Earth that had somehow colonized the wee extraterrestrial sample despite researchers' meticulous precautions. Humbled, they dutifully wrote up their findings, which were published last month. "It's a bit embarrassing," says Genge, a planetary scientist at Imperial College London. "But as a scientist, you have to tell the truth–it is important to report these things."

A Case for Careful Curation

That the grain from Ryugu offered a generous buffet for terrestrial microorganisms comes as no surprise to scientists who study such primordial asteroids, which are usually packed with carbon-rich organic molecules. The incident is instead a reminder that even the most stringent protocols can't always preclude earthly contamination. "I don't think this is a failure of the team but an inevitable consequence of doing business on Earth when working in conditions that cannot ensure sterility," says astrobiologist Andrew Steele of Carnegie Science, who was not involved with the new research. Space agencies and scientists working with the samples make every effort to avoid contamination, and that such intruders can even be spotted on a minuscule granule is a testament to the advanced technology and rigorous screening methods in place. "But ultimately we do live on a planet that is ruled by microbes, and chance events do happen," Steele says, so this episode "gives us new avenues to study and learn from."

One lesson is that changes to how a specimen is handled are risky. When Genge and his team first examined the grain in October 2022, no signs of bacteria were present, suggesting the contamination likely occurred not because of any slipup in JAXA's stringent process but rather during a necessary preparatory step in a lab at the Natural History Museum in London, where the researchers removed the grain from its container to polish it up for analysis. "We were quite careful with it, but no one was as careful as JAXA has been because we don't have the facilities," Genge says. "You only need one bacterial cell to fall on your specimen–and that's it, it's contaminated."

The case underscores "the importance of curation and that it is worth the extensive effort that we make during mission development to maintain these high standards," says JAXA's Toru Yada, who leads the sample curation for the Hayabusa2 mission and has published papers about the meticulous process. Those precautions, which also cover spacecraft construction, launch and recovery, make contamination in the agency's facilities highly unlikely, but the risk unavoidably increases once the samples are sent to scientists worldwide who don't have similar infrastructure. "And [scientists worldwide are] the ones who would make the discoveries," Genge says. "If you're misinterpreting a contaminant as part of the sample, then that becomes dangerous—you start contaminating science with incorrect hypotheses."

Genge's best guess is that the rod-shaped filaments in the Ryugu grain were from a microbe in the genus Bacillus. These hardy bacteria are known for their ability to rapidly inhabit new, extreme environments. A firm identification via DNA testing, however, was not attempted because the putative microbes were effectively trapped beneath a coating of carbon that had been applied for analysis. Several experiments on meteorites have shown that extraterrestrial material contains bountiful organics to support life as we know it, sometimes for years. But microbes can survive on so little that unless they achieve exceptionally large populations, they don't usually alter a rock's bulk composition for easy discovery by scientists. The microfossils they leave behind can be valuable tracers of their presence, but distinguishing genuine microfossils from abiotic processes that can mimic them is no easy task and has previously sparked intense debates.

"If we were to find microfossils on—insert your favorite world—it could be a potential indicator of life," says astrobiologist Manasvi Lingam of the Florida Institute of Technology, who was not affiliated with the new work. But the case of the Ryugu sample contamination shows that "if we find these structures, we have to be careful that they were not introduced by humans in some way."

Earth's Extraterrestrial Exports

Only a decade ago scientists blamed poor clean-room etiquette for allowing bacteria common in nose phlegm to sneak into NASA's Surveyor 3 spacecraft, which voyaged to the moon and had parts returned to Earth in the 1960s. Technology and protocols have greatly advanced in years since to help keep both clean rooms and our otherworldly explorations as pristine as possible. Even so, scientists will undoubtedly continue to contend with similarly difficult questions as they search for signs of alien life in samples returned from the moon, Mars and, perhaps someday, intriguing icy satellites of the outer solar system's giant planets.

If NASA's troubled Mars Sample Return (MSR) program succeeds, for instance, scientists hope to scrutinize carefully picked bits of the world to understand its prospects for life. "We are not only expecting organic rich samples but preparing for potential biosignatures," the MSR team said in a statement to *Scientific American*. "Therefore, in addition to enhanced cleaning protocols, comprehensive sterilization of the equipment and tools will be necessary–these are part of ongoing research and development efforts with our partners at [the European Space Agency]."

Closer to home, the moon is so devoid of what most organisms use for energy that microbial contamination is a minor concern for scientists working with Apollo-era lunar samples. That could change in the future if efforts such as NASA's *Artemis III* moon-sampling mission bring back materials from slightly more hospitable regions such as the ice-filled craters of the lunar south pole. All such samples would be curated in pristine environments and loaned to licensed scientists whose institutions are subject to security requirements. "NASA has been an extraordinary custodian of the Apollo samples," says geologist Darby Dyar of Mount Holyoke College, who's analyzing some of Apollo's remaining pristine samples.

Similarly, as JAXA prepares for the 2026 launch of its Martian Moons eXploration (MMX) mission to return samples from Phobos, a Martian moon, Yada says the agency has begun monitoring the environment where spacecraft is being constructed and is developing a protocol to handle the returned samples. "We publish these steps to share curation procedures with the global community ... so that researchers receiving samples can be confident in how they were handled, which is essential for interpreting scientific results," he says.

Neither agency mandates specific infrastructure or procedures for institutions loaning extraterrestrial samples, including to handle microbial contamination. "They are everywhere," Dyar says of the microbes. "From a scientific perspective, you just do the best you can." Thanks to advances in technology and screening tools, scientists are now able to study complex nuances of both biotic and abiotic chemistry at sensitivities that were unimaginable just a decade ago. Still, could we be fooled into mistaking plain old earthly microbes or their lifeless remnants for strange alien life-forms?

"It is something we in the Mars community have wrestled with for a long time," Steele says. "The short answer is no, unless alien life looks a lot like Earth life."

About the Author

Sharmila Kuthunur is an independent space journalist based in Bengaluru, India. Her work has also appeared in Science, *Space.com,* Astronomy *and Live Science, among other publications. She has earned a master's degree in journalism from Northeastern University in Boston. Follow her on BlueSky: @skuthunur.bsky.social*

Section 5: The Politics of Space Exploration

NASA Faces Deep Budget Cuts—Every Living Former Science Chief of the Agency Is Sounding the Alarm

By Rachel Feltman, Lee Billings, Fonda Mwangi, Alex Sugiura & Jeffery DelViscio

Rachel Feltman: For *Scientific American's Science Quickly*, I'm Rachel Feltman.

The White House recently proposed slashing NASA's science budget nearly in half and reducing the space agency's overall funding to just three quarters of what it received last year. When adjusted for inflation the proposed fiscal year 2026 budget would be NASA's lowest since the beginnings of the Apollo program. But these days NASA is responsible for much more than keeping up with the space race. NASA's work touches our daily lives in ways most people never realize, from the weather forecasts that help you decide what to wear to the climate data that helps farmers know when to plant their crops.

The stakes are so high that every living former NASA science chief–spanning from Ronald Reagan's administration through Joe Biden's–recently signed a letter warning that these cuts could be catastrophic for American leadership in space and science.

Today we're joined by Lee Billings, a senior editor at Scientific American who covers space and physics. He spoke with one of those former NASA science chiefs about why this moment feels different–and why the scientific community is sounding the alarm.

Lee, thanks so much for coming on to chat.

Lee Billings: It is my pleasure, as always, Rachel. I am happy to be here, even though I wish the circumstances were a bit happier.

Feltman: Right, things aren't looking great for NASA. What exactly is going on with the agency's funding?

Billings: Oof, well, to sum it up: the White House has proposed that NASA's science budget be effectively cut in half, that the agency as a whole receives about only three quarters of the funding that it received in the previous fiscal year. And there's been a lot of pushback about that, of course, because if you cut NASA's science budget in half, for instance, then you're probably gonna have to shutter, cancel, decommission dozens of active missions across the solar system and in Earth orbit, and you're going to really hamstring a lot of good science, a lot of things that feed forward into other aspects of national economies and competitiveness.

So the Senate and the House appropriators have been upset about this to various degrees, and they have, apparently, largely now restored a lot of that funding when you're looking at, like, the appropriations process and the back and forth between the Senate and the House. I don't think that we're entirely out of the woods *yet*—things are not fully finalized—but it is looking a bit brighter.

And one contributor to that pushback from Senate and House appropriators might have been a letter that was recently sent to them—an open letter from all the living previous science chiefs of NASA, the associate administrators of the Science Mission Directorate of NASA. Every single one who's still alive, from serving [in] the Reagan administration all the way through the Biden administration, signed on to this letter on a bipartisan basis and said, "We're really not cool with these proposed changes; they're potentially catastrophic for the nation and for NASA as a whole, so let's not do them."

Feltman: So this pushback is like really seriously bipartisan effort.

Billings: That's correct. And, you know, these are *serious* people. They've had their finger on the pulse of every aspect of our civil space agency for, you know, the better part of 40 years, collectively. And none of them seemed too happy about the potential changes that these budget cuts would've wrought on NASA.

Feltman: Let's talk some more about those potential changes. What are the signatories of this letter most concerned about?

Billings: You know, it–it's hard to reel out a concise laundry list because the cuts [laughs] were so large, they threatened to affect almost everything. And I'm gonna read just a couple of quick excerpts.

So they say that these budget cuts would, quote, "cede U.S. leadership in space and science to China and other nations," would "severely damage a peerless and immensely capable engineering and scientific workforce" and would "needlessly put to waste billions of dollars of taxpayer investments." They would, quote, "force the U.S. to abandon its international partners who historically contribute significantly to U.S. space science missions."

And then they spend a paragraph going into more details. And we're talking about things like winding down Hubble, even starting to wind down the James Webb Space Telescope, which only launched a few years ago. We're talking about turning off missions that are currently at Jupiter, like NASA's Juno mission. We're talking about retreating at Mars and turning off a lot of the orbiters and landers and, and rovers there.

We're also talking about closing some of NASA's eyes to Earth. We're talking about cuts that would affect things like the Landsat program, which NASA manages [with] the United States Geological Survey, which, you know, looks at things like weather and precipitation and, and helps people avoid dangerous storms or know when to plant or harvest their crops–things like that.

It even cuts into things like aeronautics; people forget that that–the first A in NASA stands for "aeronautics," I'm pretty sure, and there's lots of work that's done there, too. That's everything from developing next-generation engines and other parts of airframes that can lead to more efficient flight to, you know, software systems that can probably help air-traffic controllers and things like that. It's a full-spectrum situation.

Feltman: So I know that you talked to one of the authors of this letter. Could you tell us more about who he is and why he feels so strongly about this?

Billings: Yeah, his name's John Grunsfeld; sometimes he's called "Dr. Hubble." And he is a lot of things. In short he's an astrophysicist. He is a five-time spaceflight veteran—a former NASA astronaut who went up to fix the Hubble Space Telescope and service it, hence the "Dr. Hubble" name. And of course, he is also a former associate administrator of the Science Mission Directorate, a former chief scientist of NASA.

John Grunsfeld: There's no question that science in the United States is under attack, and the president's budget request shows that NASA, you know, is not at all spared.

Billings: And so when people like this have strong opinions and speak up I think it's important to listen. I really feel like some of his strongest material was when we prompted him by saying things like, you know, "What—why is this happening right now? What upsets you about it?" And he had some pretty sharp words for, you know, these proposals and, and the Trump administration. He threw some sharp elbows.

Grunsfeld: You know, I can only speculate that this is part of a deliberate attempt to dumb down America. People who are poorly educated are much more easily manipulated than people who have strong critical-thinking skills.

Billings: The stuff he said there, it's the kind of thing where this isn't some sign-toting hippie doing a protest in the street. Like, this guy—that was the other thing that he said that I thought was really good: when I challenged him directly, I was like, "You know, you can look through your socials and your history and I can see that, you know, you were a supporter of Kamala Harris. There's gonna be this pushback on you—that you're just a partisan hack and you're compromised by your bias—and how would you respond to that?"

And he answered me very clearly: talking about his resume, talking about his experience at NASA, talking about his spaceflights and how he put his life on the line for the nation to upgrade and service and preserve one of our most cherished and enduring iconic national resources, the Hubble Space Telescope. And he talked about how he'd worked in both Republican and Democratic administrations in the past. And, you know, I–to me that really resonated because, like, this is–he's not the kind of person who makes a lot of headlines with a lot of splashy talk, right? But when he does talk in a concerted way that's trying to get attention, I do think it's worth listening.

Feltman: Yeah, and what is he most concerned about?

Billings: So the two that he really highlighted for me when, when we spoke, the first was the cuts to astrophysics.

Grunsfeld: I'm an astrophysicist, so that actually has me seriously depressed. There's especially one cut, which is eliminating the high-altitude balloon program, which–I have to say, having run NASA Science–is probably the most efficient and productive program in all of NASA and in all of the federal government because it always has a tiny budget and it does tremendous science.

Billings: And it seems to be one of the areas where NASA and, by proxy, the United States is really in a pole position. We're really leading the world in a lot of domains of astrophysics in terms of building telescopes to see further and more clearly deeper out into the cosmos, and he definitely thinks that that is at risk.

And the other one that he pointed out has–it hits a little closer to home.

Grunsfeld: Earth science: part of NASA. And one of the things we know is that the Earth as a system is incredibly complex, and it's that view from space–not only, you know, seeing the whole Earth with our fleet of satellites but also over a long period of time–that allows us to develop models to accurately predict what the future will be.

Billings: The planet's warming, and that's not a partisan appraisal–that's just a fact. And we need to know how that works. And we need to know how it's cascading through the Earth's system to affect everything from precipitation patterns to extreme weather events, so on and so forth–sea-level rise, lots of things. So there's lots of areas where NASA's work, especially its observations of our home planet, really do touch people's lives, everyday people's lives, in, in lots of subtle ways.

Feltman: Of course NASA has faced potential budget cuts before. So, what does John say is different about this? Why did he and the rest of the folks who signed feel the need to speak out now?

Billings: One thing that's indisputable is: if you look at these proposed budget cuts and you look at NASA's funding over time, across the entirety of its nearly 70-year history, the budget cuts, if they went through, would be bringing NASA to its lowest state, its lowest budgetary state, since before the [beginnings of the] Apollo program–since, really, its founding. So that's pretty historic.

And of course, NASA is doing a lot more with its money than it did back in the Apollo days. You know, back then it was all about a moonshot and beating the Soviet Union in this new "High Frontier," and it was a very focused, almost singular goal. Now NASA's portfolio is *vast*. If you look at all the different things it's doing and all the different types of science that it supports, all the different technology development that it supports, all the different aspects of our lives that these things filter into, it's just grown so much.

So we're pairing a historically low budget with an immensely expanded portfolio of responsibilities, obligations and opportunities, and I think it's that combination that really set the alarm bells off and that really brought not just John Grunsfeld to the table to write this letter but also all of his predecessors within NASA's Science Mission Directorate.

Feltman: It makes sense that this former NASA head is really concerned about this stuff. But how could it impact our listeners?

Billings: Woo, well, I think that our listeners should care for many different reasons, and, and it kind of depends upon one's point of view. If you're really enthused and excited about just fundamentally expanding the frontiers of our knowledge about the universe, right, if you are captivated and awestruck by pretty pictures from space telescopes and other worldly vistas from interplanetary spacecraft, you should be concerned about that window closing on the universe. And again, we've been at the forefront.

Maybe you're very, very, very patriotic and you're always first to start chanting "USA!" at any public event. Well, in that case maybe you don't care so much about pretty pictures from space telescopes and rovers on Mars looking for signs of life, but maybe you just want the U.S. to be the best, right? And if these sorts of budget cuts go through, then it's very hard to see how we're still gonna be the best in these domains, instead of some other competitor nations, particularly China.

China's rapid rise in space science and exploration and spaceflight is something that many people have flagged, obviously, and that John Grunsfeld also noted when we spoke, and they are going full bore. They have a space station up there right now. They are going to be launching almost, like, a Hubble Space Telescope–like orbital observatory that's gonna hang out near their space station for servicing in [the] coming years. They are probably going to pull off the first successful Mars sample return mission before NASA and the European Space Agency, its key partner, will manage to retrieve a bunch of samples that they already have stored there on Mars.

You know, attracting the best and the brightest to our shores from all across the world, because who wouldn't want to work on a mission to land people on Mars? Who wouldn't wanna work on a mission to try to find life on some distant exoplanet? Those things are fundamentally attractive and cool to a lot of people–again, the best and the brightest–and we want to have them here, I think.

There's also the direct-utility angle of people wanting to know if it's gonna be rainy or sunny tomorrow, what they need to wear if they're going out to work: Should they wear a light sweater, or should they, you know, wear seersucker because it's gonna be 90 percent humidity? Is there gonna be a big squall or hurricane that might blow in? Those things depend on forecasts, which are based on data that, to some degree, comes from NASA assets–NASA satellites, NASA computers crunching the numbers, all that stuff. So Earth observations have a very strong, direct influence on our daily lives, whether we really recognize it or not, and it's threatened by these sorts of budget cuts.

Feltman: Lee, thank you so much for coming on to chat.

Billings: Rachel, it is always my pleasure. Again, I wish the circumstances were a little better, but hey, hope springs eternal.

Feltman: That's all for today's episode. We'll be back on Friday to talk to a meteorologist who's made his way to Washington.

Science Quickly is produced by me, Rachel Feltman, along with Fonda Mwangi, Kelso Harper and Jeff DelViscio. This episode was edited by Alex Sugiura. Shayna Posses and Aaron Shattuck fact-check our show. Our theme music was composed by Dominic Smith. Subscribe to *Scientific American* for more up-to-date and in-depth science news.

For *Scientific American*, this is Rachel Feltman. See you next time!

About the Author

Rachel Feltman is former executive editor of Popular Science *and forever host of the podcast* The Weirdest Thing I Learned This Week. *She previously founded the blog Speaking of Science for the Washington Post.*

Lee Billings is a science journalist specializing in astronomy, physics, planetary science, and spaceflight and is senior desk editor for physical science at Scientific American. *He is author of a critically acclaimed book,* Five Billion Years of

Solitude: The Search for Life Among the Stars, *which in 2014 won a Science Communication Award from the American Institute of Physics. In addition to his work for* Scientific American, *Billings's writing has appeared in the* New York Times, *the* Wall Street Journal, *the* Boston Globe, Wired, New Scientist, Popular Science *and many other publications. Billings joined* Scientific American *in 2014 and previously worked as a staff editor at* SEED *magazine. He holds a B.A. in journalism from the University of Minnesota.*

Fonda Mwangi is an award-winning multimedia editor at Scientific American *and producer of* Science Quickly. *She previously worked at* Axios, *the* Recount *and* WTOP News. *She holds a master's degree in journalism and public affairs from American University in Washington, D.C.*

Alex Sugiura is a Peabody and Pulitzer Prize–winning composer, editor and podcast producer based in Brooklyn, N.Y. He has worked on projects for Bloomberg, Axios, Crooked Media *and Spotify, among others.*

Jeffery DelViscio is currently chief multimedia editor/executive producer at Scientific American. *He is former director of multimedia at* STAT, *where he oversaw all visual, audio and interactive journalism. Before that he spent more than eight years at the* New York Times, *where he worked on five different desks across the paper. He holds dual master's degrees in journalism and in Earth and environmental sciences from Columbia University. He has worked onboard oceanographic research vessels and tracked money and politics in science from Washington, D.C. He was a Knight Science Journalism Fellow at the Massachusetts Institute of Technology in 2018. His work has won numerous awards, including two News and Documentary Emmy Awards.*

NASA Administrator Nominee Would Shift Future of Space Exploration

By Dan Vergano

In the latest turn in a battle over NASA's future, on Tuesday President Donald Trump nominated billionaire entrepreneur and private astronaut Jared Isaacman to become the agency's next administrator.

Trump had first nominated Isaacman last year. This past May he suddenly withdrew the nomination and complained of Isaacman's past campaign donations to Democratic politicians. Isaacman, now age 42, is closely associated with SpaceX's Elon Musk and has flown to space twice via the company, including in a 2024 mission that achieved the first-ever commercial space walk. Musk and Trump were at loggerheads when the president pulled Isaacman's nomination, but that political relationship is apparently now on the mend.

"Jared's passion for Space, astronaut experience and dedication to pushing the boundaries of exploration, unlocking the mysteries of the universe, and advancing the new Space economy, make him ideally suited," wrote Trump in his announcement of the renomination on his Truth Social platform. Isaacman, who had taken pains to avoid any public hint of conflict with Trump after the withdrawn nomination in May, thanked him and the space community in a social media post in response to the renomination.

The announcement came amid recent news reports that Secretary of Transportation Sean Duffy, who is NASA's acting administrator, was maneuvering to move the space agency into his Department of Transportation and remain its chief. On Monday Politico reported a 62-page "Project Athena" memo outlining Isaacman's vision for NASA, which had allegedly been shared with an undisclosed senior administration official this summer. That document advocated for radically reorganizing NASA centers across the country, outsourcing some of the space agency's science efforts and canceling the jumbo Space Launch System (SLS) rocket after the third Artemis mission to the moon. The memo also recommended that NASA pursue an ambitious program to develop nuclear-electric rockets for future human voyages to Mars, as well as cultivate more public-private partnerships to launch more lower-cost interplanetary science missions.

In a lengthy response, Isaacman pushed back against critics who portrayed the memo's call for "science as a service" as removing NASA from the Earth-observation responsibilities that are found in its charter. Instead, he said, the memo merely laid out a plan for augmenting NASA's Earth studies using the wealth of remote-sensing data available from commercial satellite firms. He said he stood by the memo, which he described as an evolving document outlining reform plans for the agency, which has long been subject to critical Government Accountability Office reports.

"I think Isaacman captured it best when he said that he got caught up in someone else's political argument," says space analyst and former NASA employee Keith Cowing, who runs the website NASA Watch. Congress and the space industry had remained interested in Isaacman's nomination over the summer, keeping his chances alive, Cowing says. "Most importantly," Cowing adds, "he was not a sore loser and thanked everyone for the opportunity and then went back to what he had been doing."

Lori Garver, a former NASA deputy administrator under the Obama administration, who has reviewed the Project Athena document, notes that while it offers plentiful "grist for the mill" for Isaacman's potential political opponents, it nonetheless "is very similar to what we had in our own transition plan" for NASA after the 2008 U.S. presidential election.

"Would it break the rice bowls of big contractors who currently get a lot of money [from NASA and] who maybe don't deliver as efficiently as they could? Absolutely," she says. "Will Congress allow that? I don't know. Right now Congress seems to allow everything the president wants–except for cutting big NASA programs."

The core concern for NASA's next leader, regardless of who that shall be, Garver says, is that they will work at Trump's behest. "This president doesn't want NASA doing any climate-change research–and that means Jared or whoever else will have to go along with that," she says. "And that's a problem because this sort of research is in NASA's charter; it's absolutely something for which the agency plays a critical role."

The renomination comes amid governmental furloughs and widespread cuts at NASA centers, including multiple rounds of layoffs at the agency's Jet Propulsion Laboratory in California and reports of lab and building closures at its Goddard Space Flight Center in Maryland. (NASA representatives did not respond to a request for comment on the legality of these shutdown closures from *Scientific American*.) NASA has fallen behind in a self-declared moon race with China, prompting a recent agency request for alternative lunar landing proposals from SpaceX, Blue Origin and other aerospace contractors.

Jack Kiraly, director of government relations for the Planetary Society, says that the Project Athena document and Isaacman's public remarks suggest that, as administrator, he would seek to boost NASA's scientific return on investment by outsourcing more work to commercial or academic partners. In principle, this would allow the agency to focus on riskier, more ambitious activities–such as building nuclear rockets or sending probes to the outer solar system–that are typically seen as beyond the reach of the private sector.

"But the thing is, NASA is already very commercialized," Kiraly says. "Previous administrators have said about 85 percent of NASA's work is done with industry. So of the 15 percent that's still done within NASA, you want to reduce that even further–while also somehow making NASA more about doing bold things only it can?"

Several agency initiatives, such as the Commercial Lunar Payload Services (CLPS) program of robotic moon landers and the Small Innovative Missions for Planetary Exploration (SIMPLEx), already rely on off-the-shelf components and the leadership of industry or academic partners. Four out of the five CLPS missions to date have failed, Kiraly notes, as have all three SIMPLEx missions that have launched so far. (A fourth, the Mars-bound Escape and Plasma Acceleration and Dynamics Explorer, or ESCAPADE, mission, is set to launch as early as next Sunday.)

"So Jared's saying NASA needs a higher tolerance for risk and needs to do more missions for less money that have a greater rate of failure," Kiraly says. "Well, is an 80 percent failure rate like for CLPS or a 100 percent failure rate like for SIMPLEx an acceptable risk posture or not? Commercialization is not necessarily a panacea, and if the plan is to repackage what NASA's already doing–just with less funding and staffing–that would fail to address the fact that NASA's workforce, and future, is under an immense amount of strain."

Privately, some former space agency officials say that Isaacman seems as good a pick for NASA as the Trump administration could deliver. While calling parts of Isaacman's Athena strategy naive or unlikely to survive contact with the space industry, one former NASA official notes that "people love that he has a strategy." In contrast, there has been no shortage of criticism for Duffy during his brief tenure, with Musk going so far as to publicly question the acting NASA chief's intelligence.

Isaacman must still face confirmation from the U.S. Senate, where influential Republican senators, such as Ted Cruz of Texas, have resisted calls to kill the SLS rocket or may question his links to SpaceX and Musk. In 1999 Isaacman made most of his fortune from founding a point-of-sale payment processing firm now known as Shift4, which serves hotels, resorts, restaurants and other leisure businesses. Shift4 made a $27.5-million investment in SpaceX in 2021, and Isaacman has spent undisclosed sums (likely hundreds of millions of dollars) on his spaceflights with the latter company. After his initial nomination, Isaacman resigned as Shift4's CEO and became its executive chairman, and he has said that, as NASA administrator, he would recuse himself from any space agency decisions involving SpaceX.

"Jared coming in could, I believe, be truly transformative—and I support that," Garver says. "But for those who don't want that transformation, it's going to be really difficult. There's no question that, with his renomination, the fight for NASA's future is now upon us."

About the Author

Dan Vergano is senior editor, Washington, D.C., at Scientific American. *He has previously written for Grid News, BuzzFeed News,* National Geographic *and* USA Today. *He is chair of the New Horizons committee for the Council for the Advancement of Science Writing and a journalism award judge for both the American Association for the Advancement of Science and the U.S. National Academies of Sciences, Engineering, and Medicine.*

NASA Budget Cuts Could End U.S. Exploration of the Outer Solar System

By Hannah Richter

In the spring of 2022 the U.S. space community selected its top priority for the nation's next decade of science and exploration: a mission to Uranus, the gassy, bluish planet only seen up close during a brief spacecraft flyby in 1986. More than 2.6 billion kilometers from Earth at its nearest approach, Uranus still beckons with what it could reveal about the solar system's early history—and the overwhelming numbers of Uranus-sized worlds that astronomers have spied around other stars. Now President Donald Trump's proposed cuts to NASA could push those discoveries further away than ever—not by directly canceling the mission but by abandoning the fuel needed to pull it off.

The technology in question, known as radioisotope power systems (RPS), is an often overlooked element of NASA's budget that involves turning nuclear fuel into usable electricity. More like a battery than a full-scale reactor, RPS devices attach directly to spacecraft to power them into the deepest, darkest reaches of the solar system, where sunlight is too sparse to use. It's a critical technology that has enabled two dozen NASA missions, from the iconic Voyagers 1 and 2 now traversing interstellar space to the Perseverance and Curiosity rovers presently operating on Mars.

But RPS is expensive, costing NASA about $175 million in 2024 alone. That's largely because of the costs of sourcing and refining plutonium 238, the chemically toxic, vanishingly scarce and difficult to work with radioactive material at the heart of all U.S. RPS. The Fiscal Year 2026 President's Budget Request (PBR) released this spring suggests shutting down the program by 2029. That's just long enough to use RPS tech on NASA's upcoming Dragonfly mission, a nuclear-powered dual-quadcopter drone to explore Saturn's frigid moon Titan. After that, without RPS, no further U.S. missions to the outer solar system would be possible for the foreseeable future.

"It was an oversight," says Amanda Hendrix, director of the Planetary Science Institute, who has led science efforts on RPS-enabled NASA missions such as Cassini at Saturn and Galileo at Jupiter. "It's really like the left hand wasn't talking to the right hand when the PBR was put together."

Throughout its 400-odd pages, the PBR repeatedly acknowledges the importance of planning for the nation's next generation of planetary science missions and even proposes funding NASA's planetary science division better than any other part of the space agency's science operations, which it seeks to cut by half. But "to achieve cost savings," it states, 2028 should be the last year of funding for RPS, and "given budget constraints and the reduced pipeline of new planetary science missions," the proposed budget provides no funding after 2026 for work by the Department of Energy (DOE) that supports RPS.

Indeed, NASA's missions to the outer solar system are infrequent because of their long durations and the laborious engineering required for a spacecraft to withstand cold, inhospitable conditions so far from home. But what these missions lack in frequency, they make up for in discovery: some of the most tantalizing and potentially habitable environments beyond Earth are thought to exist there, in vast oceans of icy moons once thought to be wastelands. One such environment lurks on Saturn's Enceladus, which was ranked as the nation's second-highest priority after Uranus in the U.S.'s 2022 Planetary Science and Astrobiology Decadal Survey.

"The outer solar system is kind of the last frontier," says Alex Hayes, a planetary scientist at Cornell University, who chaired the Decadal Survey panel that selected Enceladus. "You think you know how something works until you send a spacecraft there to explore it, and then you realize that you had no idea how it worked."

Unlike solar power systems—relatively "off-the-shelf" tech that can be used on a per-mission basis—RPS requires a continuous production pipeline that's vulnerable to disruption. NASA's program operates through the DOE, with the space agency purchasing DOE services to source, purify and encapsulate the plutonium 238 fuel, as well as to assemble and test the resulting RPS devices. The most common kind of RPS, a radioisotope thermoelectric generator, converts the thermal energy released from plutonium 238's natural decay to as much as 110 watts of electrical power. Any excess heat helps keep the spacecraft and its instruments warm enough to function.

Establishing the RPS pipeline took around three decades, and the program's roots lie in the bygone cold war era of heavy U.S. investment in nuclear technology and infrastructure. Preparing the radioactive fuel alone takes the work of multiple DOE facilities scattered across the country: Oak Ridge National Laboratory produces the plutonium oxide, then Los Alamos National Laboratory forms it into usable pellets, which are finally stockpiled at Idaho National Laboratory. Funding cuts would throw this pipeline into disarray and cause an exodus of experienced workers, Hendrix says. Restoring that expertise and capability, she adds, would require billions of dollars and a few decades more.

"These decisions are made by people that don't fully understand the implications," says Ryan P. Russell, an aerospace engineer at the University of Texas at Austin. "Technologically, [RPS] is on the critical path to superiority in space, whether that's military, civilian or industrial applications."

Russell emphasizes that RPS isn't just critical for exploring Uranus, Enceladus and other destinations in the outer solar system—it's also a likely fundamental pillar of the administration's space priorities, such as developing a sustained human presence on the moon and sending astronauts to Mars. While both destinations are relatively close to the sun, the Red Planet's global dust storms can bury solar panels, and the moon's two-week-long lunar nights are cold enough to test the mettle of even the best batteries. The latter situation informed the reasoning that drove NASA's acting administrator Sean Duffy's directive last week to fast-track a lunar nuclear reactor.

Abandoning smaller-scale nuclear options such as RPS while aiming for a full-scale reactor is "like trying to build a house without a two-by-four," Russell says. "If you don't have the basic building blocks, you're not gonna get very far."

Another initiative reliant on RPS, NASA confirmed in a statement e-mailed to Scientific American, is the beleaguered Mars Sample Return (MSR) program that the U.S. agency has been jointly pursuing with the European Space Agency. While the White House has proposed nixing MSR, scientists and politicians view bringing Martian samples back to Earth as a key milestone in the modern-day space race against China.

Meanwhile other nations are pursuing or preserving their own RPS capabilities, with Europe's sights set on americium 241, a radioisotope with a five-times-longer half-life but a five-times-weaker energy output than plutonium 238. Russia has used RPS for decades, and China and India are also developing homegrown versions of the technology.

Notably, despite the administration's push for commercial partners to take up costly space functions such as rocket launches, RPS is unlikely to find much support in the private sector. "Dealing with [this sort of] nuclear material–that's not something a company is going to do," Russell says.

Going forward, the planetary science community hopes to convince Congress that RPS is "critical and foundational," Hendrix says. The Outer Planets Assessment Group (OPAG), which was chartered by and provides independent input to NASA, expressed its concerns to the space agency in findings from a June meeting, writing that the decision would have "dire implications" for future solar system exploration. White papers prepared by representatives of the Johns Hopkins University Applied Physics Laboratory and NASA's Jet Propulsion Laboratory, Goddard Space Flight Center and Glenn Research Center conveyed similar sentiments, noting that nine of the 15 existing and future missions recommended in the latest Decadal Survey use RPS.

In short, "you're just hamstringing your ability to do certain mission configurations and also to get out to and past Saturn if you shut down RPS," Hayes says. "You can't argue that scientific prioritization was part of [the White House's] decision process."

Although both the House and Senate have released drafts of the 2026 appropriations bill that preserve top-line funding for NASA, neither explicitly mentions RPS. That means the program would fall under NASA's "discretionary spending," a category that scientists and legal experts alike say would be more easily manipulated by a presidential administration looking to enforce its political agenda. In other words, without a clear, direct callout for RPS from congressional appropriators, the Trump administration's plan to shut down the program could more easily come to pass. Hendrix consequently hopes that Congress will add language explicitly funding RPS in its final budget.

"There is a strong interest from Congress in the need for a powerful, deep-space energy source," says a congressional staffer who is familiar with the NASA budget and was granted anonymity to discuss these issues freely. But "I don't know that members have quite honed in on [RPS] yet because the worry is so much about [Trump's] intent to cancel a lot of future planetary missions."

Fundamentally, political support for outer solar system missions is a moot point without corresponding support for the ability to get there, explains University of Oregon planetary physicist and OPAG co-chair Carol Paty. The decision to shut down RPS "seems like a simple line item," she says. But the implications are "deeply troubling and concerning. If there are not big missions to drive the community, to drive exploration, to drive training the next generation, where does that leave us?"

About the Author

Hannah Richter is a freelance science journalist based in Washington, D.C. She writes about Earth, space and science policy for Science, Nature, Smithsonian, *WIRED,* Sky & Telescope, Science News, Ars Technica *and* Popular Mechanics, *among others.*

GLOSSARY

assistive technology An item or piece of equipment used to improve the functional abilities of people with disabilities.

decommissioned Something taken out of service because it's no longer needed or usable.

defibrillator A medical device that delivers an electric shock to the heart to stop dangerous rhythms or restart the heart.

deorbiting To lower a spacecraft's altitude to remove it from orbit and avoid creating space debris.

enabler A person or thing that allows someone to achieve an end.

finite Having limits.

ionize To break apart molecules to create charged particles called ions.

jettisoned To get rid of something unwanted or unneeded.

microbe A small living organism too small to be seen with the naked eye.

microgravity When gravity is so low that objects appear weightless.

mitigation To reduce the severity of something.

negligible Something so small that it can be ignored.

paradigm A standard model that determines how we understand something.

physiological Relating to normal, healthy functions of the human body.

propulsion An action or force that moves an object forward.

seismometer An instrument that detects ground motions caused by earthquakes.

stewardship The careful management of something that was trusted to someone's care.

tracheostomy A medical procedure that creates a small opening through the neck into the windpipe to provide another way for breathing.

unfettered Something free and not controlled by limitations.

FURTHER INFORMATION

Drake, Nadia. "NASA's Next Major Space Telescope Is Ready to Launch. Trump Wants to Kill It and Other Vital Science." *Scientific American*. April 18, 2025. www.scientificamerican.com/article/nasas-next-major-space-telescope-is-ready-to-launch-trump-wants-to-kill-it/.

Drake, Nadia. "White House Budget Plan Would Devastate U.S. Space Science." *Scientific American*. June 4, 2025. www.scientificamerican.com/article/proposed-federal-budget-would-devastate-u-s-space-science/.

Mogensen, Jackie Flynn. "NASA Commits to Plan to Build a Nuclear Reactor on the Moon by 2030." *Scientfic American*. January 14, 2026. www.scientificamerican.com/article/nasa-commits-to-plan-to-build-a-nuclear-reactor-on-the-moon-by-2030/.

O'Callaghan, Jonathan. "SpaceX Now has More than 10,000 Starlink Satellites in Orbit." *Scientific American*. March 17, 2026. www.scientificamerican.com/article/spacex-reaches-milestone-of-10-000-starlink-satellites-in-orbit/.

Plait, Phil. "Timekeeping on Mars Is a Tall Order. Here's Why." *Scientific American*. December 12, 2025. www.scientificamerican.com/article/what-time-is-it-on-mars/.

Scoles, Sarah. "Futuristic Radio Telescope Will Spot Baby Solar Systems–If It's Funded." *Scientific American*. May 28, 2025. www.scientificamerican.com/article/upgraded-very-large-array-telescope-will-spot-baby-solar-systems-if-its/.

Scoles, Sarah. "Why Is It So Hard to Go Back to the Moon?" *Scientific American*. September 17, 2024. www.scientificamerican.com/article/why-is-it-so-much-harder-for-nasa-to-send-people-to-the-moon-now-than-it-was-during-the-apollo-era/.

CITATIONS

1.1 Plans to Trash the Space Station Preview a Bigger Problem by Sarah Scoles (October 28, 2024); 1.2 What the Amazon versus SpaceX Satellite Mega Constellation War Means for Earth by Jonathan O'Callaghan (April 28, 2025); 1.3 Why We Need to Reduce, Reuse and Recycle in Space by Moriba Jah (January 21, 2025); 1.4 Scientists Race to Map Dangerous Ultrasmall Space Junk by Sharmila Kuthunur (July 30, 2024); 2.1 If SpaceX Goes Public in 2026, What Does That Mean for Space Exploration? by Ramin Skibba (December 26, 2025); 2.2 Why More Space Launches Could Be a Good Thing for the Climate by Riis Williams (June 7, 2024); 2.3 40 years after Challenger disaster, NASA faces safety fears on Artemis II by Meghan Bartels (January 28, 2026); 2.4 Astronauts Return to Earth in First ISS Medical Evacuation by Claire Cameron (January 15, 2026); 2.5 Crew-11 Astronauts Reflect on ISS Medical Evacuation and Future of Human Spaceflight by Claire Cameron (January 21, 2026); 2.6 NASA Evacuation of ISS Highlights How Astronauts Prepare for Medical Emergencies in Space by Claire Cameron (January 9, 2026); 2.7 Igloos on Mars? How Future Astronauts Could Use Ice to Survive by Claire Cameron (December 18, 2025); 2.8 It's Nearly Time to Say Goodbye to the International Space Station. What Happens Next? by Jonathan O'Callaghan (November 1, 2025); 2.9 Private Space Stations of the Future Promise Luxury. But Can They Deliver? by Sarah Scoles (February 26, 2025); 2.10 NASA's Perseverance Rover Faces New Uncertainty on Mars by Kendra Pierre-Louis, Lee Billings, Fonda Mwangi & Alex Sugiura (December 10, 2025); 2.11 Athena, Next U.S. Commercial Moon Lander, Is Set for Spectacular Lunar Science by Gayoung Lee (February 11, 2025); 2.12 John McFall Is Breaking Barriers as the World's First Parastronaut by Max Springer (August 20, 2024); 3.1 NASA's Artemis Astronauts Will Help Grow Crops on the Moon—And Much More by Robin George Andrews (April 17, 2024); 3.2 Is Space the Place for Earth's Next Evolutionary Leap? by Lee Billings (November 10, 2025); 3.3 Mars Can Wait. Questions Surround Settlements on Other Worlds by Mikko M. Puumala, Oskari Sivula & Kirsi Lehto (December 1, 2023); 3.4 Can We Even Have Babies in Space? Why We're Not Ready for Life Off-Planet by Clara Moskowitz (November 9, 2023); 3.5 Are We Ready for Death in Space? by Peter Cummings (June 4, 2025); 4.1 Human Missions to Mars Must Search for Alien Life, New Report Finds by Lee Billings (December 9, 2025); 4.2 The Search for Extraterrestrial Life Is a Roller Coaster of Hope and Disappointment by Sarah Scoles (August 19, 2025); 4.3 Scientists Discover Earth Life inside an Asteroid Sample by Sharmila Kuthunur (December 19, 2025); 5.1 NASA Faces Deep Budget Cuts—Every Living Former Science Chief of the Agency Is Sounding the Alarm by Rachel Feltman, Lee Billings, Fonda Mwangi, Alex Sugiura & Jeffery DelViscio (August 6, 2025); 5.2 NASA Administrator Nominee Would Shift Future of Space Exploration by Dan Vergano (November 5, 2025); 5.3 NASA Budget Cuts Could End U.S. Exploration of the Outer Solar System by Hannah Richter (August 14, 2025).

INDEX

P

R

S

Z